The Mystery of Christ

The Mystery of Christ

Guy Appéré

 EVANGELICAL PRESS

EVANGELICAL PRESS
16/18 High Street, Welwyn, Herts AL6 9EQ, England

© Evangelical Press 1984

*First published in French under the title "Le Mystère de Christ",
(Editions Grâce et Vérité, 1980)
First English edition, 1984*

Translated from the French by Alan and Simone Gibb.

ISBN 0 85234 180 6

*Typeset in Great Britain by Herts Typesetting Services Ltd.
Printed by The Pitman Press, Bath, England.*

I want you to know
how much I am struggling
for you
and for those at Laodicea,
and for all who have not met me personally.

My purpose is that they may be encouraged in heart
and united in love,
so that they may have the full riches of complete
understanding,

in order that they may know the *mystery* of God,
namely, *Christ*,
in whom are hidden
all the treasures of wisdom and knowledge.

Paul

Contents

Preface

This little book does not claim to be a full commentary, but something far more modest: a series of short meditations — which have kept much of their original character as talks — on one of the most concise and complete epistles written by the apostle Paul.

Written in response to the problems of a small church in Asia Minor during the first century A.D., it is still highly relevant in this modern age of dissatisfaction and moral confusion. The solution it offers in such situations, be they past or present, is not some heroic spiritual effort to rise above oneself, but the divine person of Jesus Christ, in whom we are made complete by virtue of his work of redemption. This letter, while showing great pastoral concern, is also a masterpiece of critical argument.

The author wishes to acknowledge the invaluable help he has found in J.B.Lightfoot's commentary *(Saint Paul's Epistles to the Colossians and to Philemon, 1897)*, and also in parts of commentaries by A. Vinet *(Etudes et méditations évangéliques, 1841)* and N. Hugedé *(L'Epître aux Colossiens, 1968)*.

Guy Appéré

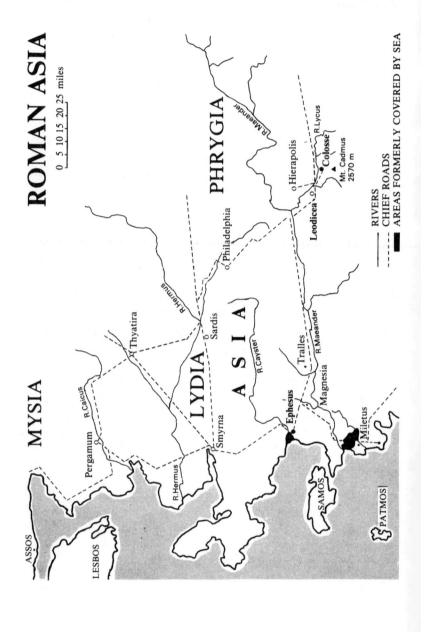

ROMAN ASIA

0 5 10 15 20 25 miles

MYSIA

PHRYGIA

LYDIA

ASIA

ASSOS

LESBOS

Pergamum

R.Caicus

R.Hermus

Thyatira

Smyrna

Sardis

R.Hermus

R.Cayster

Philadelphia

Tralles

R.Maeander

Magnesia

Ephesus

Miletus

SAMOS

PATMOS

Hierapolis

R.Lycus

Colosse

Mt. Cadmus
2570 m

Leodicea

R.Maeander

——— RIVERS
- - - - CHIEF ROADS
▓▓▓ AREAS FORMERLY COVERED BY SEA

1.
Introduction

The Lycus Valley churches

Some 125 miles east of Ephesus in Asia Minor, along the banks of a small river called the Lycus, and situated at roughly ten-mile intervals were three towns, the names of which have been preserved in the Bible: Laodicea, Hierapolis and Colosse (Col. 4:13). These towns had much in common; among other things, all three were situated on the well-known earthquake line. All too often their geographical position and their history have been changed by earthquakes.

Laodicea had grown rich because of its woollen industry and well-developed trade. In the book of Revelation, the letter that the apostle John writes as from the Lord to the church in Laodicea mentions this wealth and its unfortunate spiritual consequences. The citizens were so rich that they were able to rebuild the whole town without any outside help after a terrible earthquake[1] had reduced it to a heap of ruins.

Hierapolis, on the other side of the Lycus, was also a large and prosperous city. It was a spa and holiday resort, frequented by people of wealth and leisure and by invalids in search of a cure. But Hierapolis was also, as its name implies, a 'holy city', in fact it was one of the great centres of pagan mysticism in the Roman province of Asia.

Finally, there was *Colosse*, a mere village compared with its two large and wealthy neighbours. It had been an important town a few centuries earlier, but the political dominance of Laodicea and the growing popularity of Hierapolis had con-

[1] In A.D. 60 according to Tacitus; in 64 or 65 if we accept Eusebius' account.

siderably reduced its importance, and it was soon to be wiped off the map and heard of no more[2]. Despite its name, Colosse was certainly the smallest church to which the apostle Paul wrote a letter. Indeed, while the churches in Laodicea and Hierapolis would still be spoken of long afterwards, Colosse would disappear completely from church history.

These three towns had received the gospel and within them there had sprung up a small group of churches, watched over with loving devotion by Epaphras (4:12–16).

The church in Colosse

Unlike many other churches, the one in Colosse was probably not founded by the apostle Paul; indeed, he apparently had not met the brothers in Christ to whom he was writing (2:1), and, besides, none of his missionary journeys seems to have taken him to these parts.

It was probably Epaphras, a Colossian, who first preached the gospel there (1:6–8). This faithful servant of God and companion of Paul must have been converted through the ministry of the apostle, who had spent three years in Ephesus. This town was the capital of the region called Asia in which Colosse was situated. Paul's preaching had spread so widely that 'all the Jews and Greeks who lived in the province of Asia heard the word of the Lord' (Acts 19:10). The silversmith Demetrius, furious at the way his trade was being threatened by the success of the gospel, gave incontrovertible evidence of this success in his speech to his fellow craftsmen: 'You see and hear how this fellow Paul has convinced and led astray large numbers of people here in Ephesus and in practically the whole province of Asia. He says that man-made gods are no gods at all' (Acts 19:26).

[2] Shortly after the epistle was written, Colosse was totally destroyed by the same earthquake that devastated Laodicea and probably Hierapolis. It was rebuilt about a mile away but even smaller. Today it is known as Honaz.

It was also through Epaphras, who was staying with Paul at the time this letter was written, that Paul got to know the Colossian church (1:4,8,9). Epaphras had brought good news of his group of churches (1:3–8), and yet he was somewhat concerned: for false teaching had crept in and brought with it the wrong practices which always accompany it.

Though it had so far stood firm, the church in Colosse was in danger of being led astray by those who, without consciously denying or belittling the gospel, wanted to improve on it and put forward additions to the apostolic doctrine preached by Epaphras; according to them, the observance of certain practices and the possession of supposedly superior knowledge would lead the Colossian Christians onto a higher spiritual plane. This danger of syncretism which threatened the churches of that time — the attempt to combine with the gospel religious doctrines or practices of other origins — is still with us today. It is the typical temptation of our modern age which is so characterized by theological relativism and tolerance of all systems of religion.

We can identify the various influences at work in the church of Colosse by examining the allusions Paul makes to them, as he condemns error or suggests remedies. First, there was *the influence of the Judaizers*, leading the young churches of pagan origin towards a legalism characterized by the observance of Jewish practices, holy days and festivals (2:11–17), as we know had happened with serious consequences in Galatia; and secondly, *the influence of the Greek environment*, with its philosophical speculations regarding the ordering of the universe, its ascetic practices and its superstitious beliefs (2:8, 18–23).

The Epistle to the Colossians

To counter the infiltration of the church by these subtle influences, Paul has just one argument: Jesus Christ. It is in Christ that man is made complete (1:27, 28, NASB).

Nothing exists outside of, or in addition to the person and the work of Jesus Christ, who is the fulness of God (1:19; 2:9). All that we can ever have, or know, or be is in Christ. He is the reality; all else is but a shadow (2:17); all super-knowledge or super-spirituality is mere deception (2:8); any 'improvement' on the gospel is in fact a backward step; any addition to Christ is really to diminish him; all contempt for the body is sin against the spirit. All things were created by Christ and for Christ and it is only when we give him the first place in creation, in the church and in the life of the Christian (1:16–18) that everything falls into its proper place and all problems are finally solved.

The apostle's message to the church in Colosse is still very relevant today. Indeed, how many Christians when, in all humility, they consider God's greatness and their own insignificance, feel unworthy to approach him, and convince themselves that he could never condescend to speak to them! So, like the Colossians, they wish they could find some means, however difficult, of bridging the gap which separates them from God, or that they could be intiated into some more sophisticated doctrine which would make this possible.

It is true that God is great — far greater than we can imagine. It is true that we are incapable and unworthy of communicating with him — even more so than we think. But nothing and no one can open the way to God, except Jesus Christ, our only mediator. Being, at one and the same time, both God and man, he has bridged the immense gulf which separated us from an infinitely holy God. He spoke to us men *from* God, and now speaks on our behalf *to* the one who is henceforth 'our Father in heaven'. Only he could do this work, and he has done it perfectly. There is therefore nothing to be added to it.

Men have always tried, consciously or unconsciously, and often with an eye to their own glory or advantage, to interpose mediators between the human soul and God: angels or men, theologians or priests, saints or visionaries, who have taken the place of God — or very nearly! Jesus Christ, at once above all things (1:15–17) and within us (1:27), is the great answer to these human deviations.

Thus the theme of the Epistle to the Colossians is *Jesus Christ*, 'the image of the invisible God', the mystery 'in whom are hidden all the treasures of wisdom and knowledge'. It is 'in him' that 'you have been made complete'.

2.
The apostle and the church

Please read Colossians 1:1–2

The author and his companion

Paul did not found the Colossian church, nor did he have pastoral care over it. He nevertheless took a keen interest in its joys and sorrows. He was gladdened by the good news which reached him and joyfully thanked God for it, but he was also greatly distressed to hear of the heresy threatening the church: 'Now I rejoice in my sufferings for your sake' (1:24,NASB).

As an apostle, Paul felt responsible for the church as a whole — not only for the churches in Philippi, Corinth or Ephesus which he founded and which were his particular responsibility. His concern was for the whole church and he suffered for it both spiritually and physically.

We are not Paul, we are not apostles; nevertheless, do we not need to broaden our vision, our affections and our prayers so as to reach beyond the limits of our local church and to feel responsible for a wider ministry? This should not be the concern of just a few Christians, but of each one of us. The church in Colosse had probably grasped this truth, for Paul thanks God for the love which the Colossians had 'for all the saints' (1:4).

'**Paul, an apostle of Christ Jesus**.' He was the messenger of Jesus Christ, the bearer of the good news of eternal salvation in Christ. He did not stand for a church, an idea or an ideology, any more than he founded a religion or 'distorted' the teaching of Jesus, as some have accused him of doing. He was sent by God to interpret Jesus in accordance with God's own mind, to make known to us 'the glorious riches of this mystery, which is Christ in you, the hope of glory' (1:27).

Did Paul derive a feeling of pride from this extraordinary privilege? Not at all. He could detect no personal merit in himself which might have moved God to choose him. If he was an apostle, it was '**by the will of God**', by his grace alone; it did not come from himself, from a personal intention or desire to serve God, but from an irresistible call, a divine imperative which had nothing to do with him or any other human being (Gal. 1:15–20; 2:5–9). He was certainly set apart by men in the church at Antioch, but they were acting in obedience to God when they sent off Paul and Barnabas (Acts 13:1–3).

Thus Paul held his authority direct from God; he was the messenger of Jesus Christ, not the representative of a church. That accounts for all the power of his astonishing ministry. He never set out of his own accord, he never put forward his own ideas, or cultivated his own popularity; since he expected to receive nothing from men he never tried to please them, and his preaching was always free from human restrictions. He was the servant of Jesus Christ, 'the apostle of Jesus Christ by the will of God' alone.

But the magnitude of his ministry did not condemn the apostle to loneliness and isolation, and never got in the way of warm and loyal friendships. On the contrary, though 'free and belong[ing] to no man' (1 Cor. 9:19), he always managed to gather a devoted band of companions around him. He, the apostle of Jesus Christ, was at the heart of a team. In fact, when we study the missionary activity of the first century, we find that while the rapid spread of Christianity was, of course, due to the witness of all the Christians (Acts 8:4), and to the ministry of the apostles in particular, it also resulted from the work of a team co-ordinated by the Holy Spirit.

In the letter to the Colossians the name of Timothy appears beside that of the apostle: '**and Timothy our**

brother'. But he was not the only team member to accompany the tireless traveller; other companions were Silas, Luke, Titus, Mark, Priscilla and Aquila. When he had to leave Philippi, Paul probably entrusted the work to Luke[1]; Timothy had to carry it on in Thessalonica (1 Thess. 3:2,6), then with Silas in Berea (Acts 17:14); a few years later Titus was made responsible for organizing the churches in Crete (Titus 1:5). While a rearguard was building up and strengthening the new communities in this way, an advance party was preparing the apostle's way elsewhere: the friendly tent-makers, Aquila and his wife Priscilla, took on this task in Ephesus and Rome in particular (Acts 18:18,19; Rom. 16:3–5).

'Timothy our brother' represents here all these servants of God who, though less well known than Paul, worked with him in spreading and implanting the gospel throughout the Roman Empire. He, too, shares in the joys and sufferings of the apostle and of the church in Colosse, and joins in the thanksgiving and prayer which open this epistle.

The Colossians

'**To the saints and faithful brethren in Christ who are at Colosse**' (NASB). Those to whom the letter is addressed are called 'saints' and 'brothers'. The first of these terms describes the Christians in their relationship with God and the world, the second in their relationship with one another.

'*Saints.*' Most people think of a saint as someone who has attained perfection, that is, a state of perfect holiness. But Paul uses this word in its Old Testament meaning: set apart, marked off, dedicated to God. In biblical language, a saint is

---

[1] Luke, who sets off with Paul from Troas ('we', Acts 16:11), does not seem to be with him when he leaves Philippi ('they' Acts 17:1). They travel together again when Paul comes through Philippi once more seven or eight years later ('we', Acts 20:6).

one who is separated from the world and dedicated to the service of God and is therefore aiming at perfection. The apostle Paul himself wrote, 'Not that I have already ... been made perfect, but I press on ... to win the prize' (Phil. 3:12–14).

However, there is a sense in which we are already perfect and Paul may have been thinking of this aspect of holiness when writing his letter. For 'in Christ' we are indeed holy. When by faith we were united with Jesus, his holiness became ours. 'In Christ', God can look upon us as holy. That is what we call 'justification'.

We should note that in the Bible the word 'saint' never occurs in the singular. Holiness cannot be a private virtue, a solitary exercise: it is together, and in Jesus Christ, that we are saints, and it is together that we must seek holiness.

Separated from the world, dedicated to God: that is what the first term suggests, while at the same time preparing us for the second.

'Brothers'. This follows on logically from the idea of being set apart. True, God has separated us from the world, but in doing so he has brought us into a family, for the Christian is by nature and calling a 'brother'.

This word 'brother' also means that the Christian cannot be a law unto himself or 'go it alone'. He is not made for solitude but for solidarity, and this solidarity must show itself in a practical way. It is not enough for him to say that he belongs to the universal, spiritual church. Although such a bond is of prime importance, it is not enough in itself. The Christian must be truly a brother, that is to say he must give and receive, love and be loved, weep with those who weep, rejoice with those who rejoice; he must also seek God's will in company with his brothers and accept the need for a common discipline within the local spiritual family to which he belongs. Within this framework brotherly relationships can grow in practical ways. That is why it is a privilege to be connected with a church, or better still, to be a church member.

But brotherhood, like holiness, can only exist in Christ: 'brothers *in Christ*'. If we seek this brotherhood outside Christ we are in for big disappointments. To look for it in line with our own tastes and affinities within a particular social group having common interests or inclinations is to invite failure. We can choose our friends, but not our brothers; just as these are 'given' to us in the human family, they are also given to us 'in Christ'. Whatever we may think, they are the best and most useful for our eternal good. God's choice is always the best. Not only *must* we live with them, but we *cannot* live without them!

3.
Faith, love and hope

Please read Colossians 1:3–8

The letter opens on a note of thanksgiving, even though its main concern is admonition. This approach is typical of the apostle Paul, who always makes it his duty to present the truth — even the most unpalatable truth — in love (Eph. 4:15; 2 Tim. 2:25).

In the apostle's constant prayer for the Colossians there wells up spontaneous thankfulness for his brothers, unknown to him by sight but beloved in Jesus Christ. Despite their imperfections and mistakes, Paul still sees their good qualities and, in particular, God's wonderful grace at work in them. He does not dwell on their faults: **'We always thank God, the Father of our Lord Jesus Christ, when we pray for you**.' In fact there can be no prayer without thanksgiving and no thanksgiving without prayer. Prayer and thanksgiving should always go hand in hand.

Let us note in passing that although the apostle was far away from the church at Colosse and did not know it well, he nevertheless cared and struggled for it — in prayer. Prayer today seems to be an undervalued ministry. It is not so conspicuous as preaching, evangelization or mission, and we do not often credit it with results because these are not always seen. It is a humble, hidden ministry, and yet a most necessary one!

How much fruit it bears, perhaps unknown to us! How many victories are due to it! No doubt it is through the preaching of great men that the gospel has been carried to the farthest corners of the earth, but is it not also thanks to the prayers of countless humble children of God? So the

Christians in Colosse, who had never met Paul, owed much to his ministry of prayer.

But for what was the apostle giving thanks? For the harvest produced by the gospel in Colosse. The gospel, faithfully preached by Epaphras, had filled the hearts of the Colossians with a firm *hope* which upheld and maintained the *love* and *faith* of the church.

In the First Epistle to the Corinthians (13:13), these three gospel graces are placed in ascending order of importance: faith, hope and love. But elsewhere (1 Thess. 1:3; 5:8) and especially in the epistle we are now studying, they are put in logical order: faith which rests on the past, love which is at work in the present, hope which embraces the future.

Faith

Firstly, faith is given here its rightful place at the start of Christian experience. Faith is a necessary condition for love and hope, although hope is presented as the stimulus to both love and faith: '**the faith and love that spring from the hope that is stored up for you in heaven**'. While hope is logically the result of faith, faith in turn is sustained, renewed and revitalized by hope. This is the sense in which the passage presents hope as a source rather than an end result.

The faith of the Colossians, like all real faith, is not simply a belief in Jesus Christ. Nor is it the static faith which goes with mechanical repetition of the creed, nor a faith born of the intellect alone which believes in the existence of God and Jesus Christ. It is not even just a faith in a being beyond ourselves whom we can know, contemplate and love, as we would a person whose love for us we have come to realize. When Paul speaks of faith 'in' Jesus Christ, it is not merely a faith directed towards Jesus, but one which is lived *in* Jesus. It is a living faith which, so to speak, moves, develops and grows 'in Jesus Christ'.

Only a faith like this can keep us from error in all its forms, both in doctrine and practice. A perfectly orthodox creed or confession of faith is not in itself a sufficient safeguard. This is evidenced by the fact that many churches, who still recite the Apostles' Creed — an affirmation of faith in complete conformity with the gospel – no longer always believe or live out the truth which it expresses.

Only a faith lived 'in Christ', a living faith sustained by real fellowship with Jesus Christ, is strong enough to resist the encroachment of rationalism and meet the need for holiness in the churches. The readers of this letter were inspired by faith of this quality. That is why Paul was able to thank God, in the certainty that it would defeat the insidious heresy threatening the very existence of the church in Colosse (Rev. 2:4,5).

Love

'**Love for all the saints**' is the second gospel grace evident in the lives of the Colossians. Love is the vital and natural complement of faith. Paul writes to the Galatians of 'faith expressing itself through love'. Faith and love are inseparable.

Real faith, faith that is living in its very nature, is also living in the results it produces. As James reminds us in his epistle, 'Faith by itself, if it is not accompanied by action, is dead ... As the body without the spirit is dead, so faith without deeds is dead' (James 2:17, 26). It is impossible for faith in Jesus Christ to remain on the theoretical, mystical, heavenly or 'spiritual' plane; it expresses itself in love in a practical way. Today some people preach love without faith, but in that case it cannot be the love of which the gospel speaks.

The love we are now considering originates in God, it is the expression of our faith 'in Jesus Christ'; it is guided by

the wisdom of faith and renewed by its power. Love without
faith belongs to the human sphere; generally it is selective
and has certain favoured objects, it weakens and sometimes
dies, it does not always withstand disappointment,
ingratitude and the ravages of time! Only love rooted 'in
God', who himself is love (1 John 4:8), has the characteristics
of true love so beautifully described in the First Epistle to the
Corinthians.

It is this vital force springing from faith which makes it
possible to love 'all the saints'. Philanthropy is not necessarily love, and often what goes under the name of 'love' today
is really a denial or a caricature of it.

The love of the Colossians is the fruit of a living faith and
of life 'in Jesus Christ'; it is the expression of the life of the
Spirit in them: 'Epaphras . . . told us of your love in the
Spirit.' But if it is to survive and to triumph over all the trials
and disappointments which beset it, this love needs the third
fruit of the gospel: hope.

Hope

' . . . **That spring from the hope that is stored up for you
in heaven**.' While love springs from faith, it is sustained by
hope: it is hope that encourages, renews and revitalizes it
and gives it its eternal dimension.

Love always hopes (1 Cor. 13:7). If there were no hope,
love would soon evaporate and turn to bitterness. Hope,
towards which faith and love are leading, is also the source of
their renewal. God has set in the heart of man the thought of
eternity (Eccl. 3:11), a sense of the infinite, and only the
hope proclaimed by the gospel can satisfy this need for the
absolute. Without this hope the world is devoid of meaning
and purpose, as the present-day atheist philosophers have
clearly seen. Without it everything collapses, even faith and
love. 'If only for this life we have hope . . ., we are to be

pitied more than all men' (1 Cor. 15:19). Only this hope can satisfy the Christian's present longing for knowledge, purity, strength and perfection, which are unattainable in this life. It alone helps him to love his brothers until they reach perfection together.

But how could the Christians in Colosse have received faith, love and hope unless the gospel, the word of truth, had been preached to them? These graces are all fruits produced by the gospel and it is to the gospel that Paul now draws our attention.

The gospel, the word of truth

'**The hope ... that you have already heard about in the word of truth, the gospel that has come to you**.' We notice here how Paul stresses that it is not only necessary for the gospel to be preached, but that it should be preached in accordance with the truth. The gospel is called '*the word of truth*', and the Colossians 'understood God's grace *in all its truth*' through the faithful ministry of Epaphras. Paul probably wants to emphasize the contrast between the gospel that was preached to them at the beginning and the one they are now hearing from the lips of false teachers.

The truth must be preached '*in truth*', that is, according to its nature: it must be preached honestly, in its totality (not a truncated, expurgated, adapted gospel), and in a balanced way (not singling out some particular aspect of the truth which happens to fit in with our preferences or temperament).

This gospel is the good news of '*the grace of God*'. For it reveals that our salvation has been given and fully worked out by God — not so much to answer a call from man as to fulfil God's need to love and show his grace. We have not come to the gospel; it has come to us!

It was this gospel too which gave the Colossians the hope

which upheld their faith and love, for without the gospel there is no hope. The natural order of things gives us no grounds for hope: it bears a message of death. The gospel brings the only true, steadfast and reasonable hope for the world at all times and in all places.

'**All over the world this gospel is producing fruit**.' Everywhere, the apostle seems to be saying, the gospel has been equal to the situation and has been powerfully at work; everywhere it is relevant and bears fruit. This adaptability of the gospel is certainly one of the marks of its divine origin. For false religions were usually limited in time or space, they were often restricted to a well-defined geographical, historical or social setting, whereas the gospel is equally well fitted to Western and Eastern temperaments, to Jew and Gentile, to the cultured and the uncivilized, to the twentieth and first centuries.

Everywhere the gospel '**is producing fruit and growing**' like a healthy tree. It carries within itself the principle of its own propagation. That is what explains the extraordinary spread of Christianity during the first century by means which were out of all proportion to the results. Everywhere it brought faith, love and hope. Everywhere it continues to bring them today for the salvation of men and the glory of God.

4.
Knowledge and practice

Please read Colossians 1:9–11

Whenever Paul prayed for the Colossians he thanked God. Indeed, the little church in Colosse certainly seems to have had its good qualities. The truth, faithfully preached, had yielded a precious and abundant harvest, and the three gospel graces — faith, love and hope — were flourishing.

But the apostle was not writing to the Colossians just to compliment them! He had great ambitions for this church and wanted to see it grow in knowledge and good works, for it was essential that it should move forward into maturity if it was to withstand the false teachers and false prophets trying to foist their pseudo-philosophy upon it. The real antidote to error is a Christianity that is alive. Never in biblical language do 'falsehood' and 'truth' belong to the realm of ideas or theories! Both truth and falsehood are powers, powers of life or of death.

What, then, is the apostle's prayer? For the Christians in Colosse he asks two things which are in fact connected: a better *knowledge* of God and of his will, and a Christian *life* following from it.

Knowledge

'**Asking God to fill you with the knowledge of his will through all spiritual wisdom and understanding**.' This is Paul's prayer for the Colossians, and he adds later, '**growing in the knowledge of God**'.

Ignorance is the mother of all superstition. Those who

despise knowledge, thinking that living out the gospel only consists of doing things, are cutting themselves off from the real motive for this activity, from the principles which inspire and guide it. Also, if we think the gospel has nothing to do with the intellect but only involves the emotions, we are sadly mistaken.

'To know Christ' is for Paul the greatest privilege, the goal he is always striving for. Knowledge is the basis of salvation: 'Faith comes from hearing the message, and the message is heard through the word of Christ' (Rom. 10:17). It is the essence of salvation: 'This is eternal life: that they may know you' (John 17:3). It is the principle of growth: 'Growing in the knowledge of God' (1:10). It is the goal of the Christian life: 'Then I shall know fully, even as I am fully known' (1 Cor. 13:12).

But it is also true that we only know in part and that in this life our knowledge will always be incomplete. So we shall never be fully satisfied and we must continually remind ourselves of this so as to remain humble in our relationship with God and with our brothers. This relationship must also be one of love, because the fragment of eternal truth which *we* know is not necessarily the part our brother has grasped! So we in the church must be tolerant and learn from each other, so that together we may grow in the knowledge of God.

It is possible for knowledge to 'make arrogant' (1 Cor. 8:2). Paul puts the Corinthians on their guard against this fault, but he explains immediately that 'The man who thinks he knows something does not yet know as he ought to know' (1 Cor. 8:2; cf. 1 Cor. 13:2). True knowledge is humble and goes hand in hand with love: the Bible does not separate one from the other. In his first letter to the Corinthians, Paul sees love as a counterbalance to the misuse of knowledge, and in his letter to the Philippians he sees knowledge as a corrective to misguided love: 'This is my prayer: that your love may abound more and more in knowledge and depth of insight, so that you may be able to discern what is best' (Phil. 1:9). In other words, knowledge is not truly knowledge if it lacks love, and love is not truly love if it lacks knowledge. Knowledge without love is barren, indeed it is dangerous; love without knowledge is blind and equally barren.

It is not just any knowledge that Paul wishes the Colossians to have, but the knowledge *of God*. There is nothing theoretical or speculative about it; nor is it the privilege of an initiated few, like the knowledge that the false teachers were trying to introduce. It does not get lost in a maze of hypotheses or systems; it is a practical knowledge: 'I want to know Christ and the power of his resurrection and the fellowship of sharing in his sufferings' (Phil. 3:10). The knowledge Paul speaks of comes from fellowship — in fact it *is* fellowship with God.

But the apostle goes further: 'the knowledge *of his will*'; not only the knowledge of God himself, infinitely precious and infinitely wonderful though that is, but of his will: what is his plan for me, what does he want of me? To know God and to know his will! These are the two great questions in life. They are the ones which came spontaneously to the lips of the great apostle to the Gentiles at the time of his conversion on the Damascus road: 'Who are you, Lord?' and 'What shall I do, Lord?'

Even though knowledge of the person of God is a mystery too deep for us to fathom, it is always possible to know his will. This is within our reach, for God has promised not to leave us in the dark about it. Anyone who 'chooses to do his will' can be confident of knowing it (John 7:17).

We should realize that such knowledge requires wisdom and understanding: '*through all spiritual wisdom and understanding*', but Paul makes it clear that these are 'spiritual', that is, given by the Spirit. However, the gifts of the Spirit certainly do not preclude toil and hardship; Paul one day received a definite call to 'come over into Macedonia' (Acts 16:9), but he also had to learn through suffering that he was meant to stay some time in Galatia (Acts 16:6; Gal. 4:13).

Knowledge of God's will is the joint work of his Word and

Spirit within us, and this work shows itself in wisdom and understanding through our own faculties of reason and judgement. God's Word, our circumstances and our thoughts need to be carefully examined and weighed up before him in meditation and prayer, patience and humility. God, who has given us everything (2 Peter 1:3), will not allow us to be passive; he wants our whole being to be involved actively (2 Peter 1:5). That is why this precious gift, the knowledge of the will of God, will be expressed through our own faculties of thought, enlightened, guided and inspired by the Spirit.

Practice

This knowledge of God has its application in everyday life: **'That you may live a life worthy of the Lord and may please him in every way, bearing fruit in every good work, ... being strengthened with all power according to his glorious might.'**

Practice depends on knowledge. It is not possible to live a life worthy of the Lord unless we know him and know his will. The Christian life, far from being the realization of our own plans, our own ambitions and our own will, is meant to put *God's* plan into practice, with the resources he gives us, at the times he wishes.

The Christian life is not even serving God, praying to him and worshipping him in what *we* honestly believe is the right way. The Christian life is not to bring God into our designs, our plans, our thoughts, our work, our life, our service; no, it is to enter into *his* design, *his* service, *his* work, *his* plans, it is to try to 'please him in every way': 'Lord, what do you want me to do? All I want is to please you, but how can I do that? I could think of many ideas you might like, but what do you really want, Lord?' Have we never had the experience of giving a present, only to disappoint the person we were trying to please? Do we not sometimes disappoint our God by giving him something he never wanted, by carrying out a task he never asked us to do? To please God means to follow his revealed will, it means to obey.

How we need to be 'strengthened with all power according to his glorious might' if we are to live a life worthy of Christ! To know God and to have his power are the two essentials of a life which glorifies him and is fully pleasing to him.

But glorifying God is inseparable from our duty to serve men. For how can anyone say he loves God if he does not love his brother? (1 John 4:20.) True knowledge of God and a life pleasing to him find their natural expression '*in every good work*'. It would be impossible to make a list of all such good deeds, for knowledge of God — which itself is love — gives the Christian an inventive mind able to think of more and more new forms of service.

Christianity is practical. The apostle James brings this home to us quite clearly: what we do is proof of our faith, and if our good deeds are few and far between it is because we do not know God as we should! 'Show me your deeds and I will believe in your faith,' people are entitled to say to us. 'Faith without deeds is dead' (James 2:15–18, 26; cf. 1 John 3:17).

From among all the possible practical outworkings of faith, Paul chooses two: endurance, or perseverance, and patience. As if these were not demanding enough, he emphazises 'always', and to all this he adds 'joyfully giving thanks': 'So that you may have great endurance and patience, ... joyfully giving thanks'. Endurance and patience, especially when combined with joyful thanksgiving, show that faith is real.

Let us note that the 'glorious might' of God finds its expression particularly in these two 'passive' virtues, rather than in active qualities or exceptional deeds. It is in times of testing that the true extent of endurance and patience can be seen. *Endurance* here means not giving way to discouragement, not going to pieces when weighed down with troubles, and *patience* is being able to endure wrongs without taking revenge, without retaliating.

Surely it is in such circumstances that a man's real character shows up. And when thanksgiving with joy is added to endurance and patience, do we not see God's glorious power shining through in the sufferer's life? These two qualities, therefore, are not simply passive: joyful thanksgiving gives to endurance and patience their triumphant nature. There is no longer any question of resignation, still less of indifference or apathy: we are seeing the triumph of faith, the triumph of the glorious power of God in a human life.

This is where growth in the knowledge of God should lead us. It will no longer be a sterile, conceited knowledge, but real communion with God, in which his grace will be manifested fully as it is imparted to us in our weakness.

5.
The kingdom

Please read Colossians 7:12–14

Step by step we are being brought near to the person of Christ, the image of the invisible God, the Creator of all things, the Head of the church, the manifestation of the Godhead, the King of creation, the Prince of the eternal kingdom. Paul will soon introduce him to us, for it is in him that the Colossians are to find the answer to their problems.

But before we see the *King*, we have a description in majestic language of the *kingdom* and its subjects. How different from the language used by the heretics in Colosse (as can be detected through the words of the epistle or reading between the lines), and even from that of many Christians (or so-called Christians) of all centuries, who have a limited idea of Christianity, who live and move in the stuffy atmosphere of their own narrow little world, and for whom *life* amounts to nothing more than the use of certain pious phrases and dignified gestures, a petulant insistence on certain points of dogma, a self-satisfied sectarianism and punctilious attention to certain rituals! This is certainly not the impression made on us by these words of the apostle Paul which convey such a sense of greatness, wealth and infinity! How broad, how vast, the sweep of the apostle's thought!

He again thanks God (1:3), inviting his readers to join him in praise for the Christian's glorious inheritance. Similarly, instead of losing our way in all kinds of abstruse philosophical theories or legalistic practices, as the Colossians were tempted to do, let us fix our eyes on the boundless horizons of the kingdom to which we are heirs, and wonder at the glory of its King. That is the tonic Paul offers us. Leaving

behind in the valley the mists and ravines of 'religion', he
leads us towards the summits, from where we shall be able to
glimpse the beauty of God's kingdom and shout for wonder
and thankfulness.

Heirs

'**The Father ... has qualified you to share in the inheritance.**' So salvation is not simply release from sin. It means
all the riches of an eternal, infinite inheritance unequalled by
anything else. Nothing can be on a small scale with God!

The gospel does not only offer us forgiveness for our sins —
with which some people are content — it opens up to us all
the resources of God. It speaks to us of pardon, certainly, but
also of hidden treasure, of a pearl of great value (Matt.
13:44–46), of a royal banquet (Matt. 22:2–14), of a wedding
feast (Mark 2:19).

True, the full measure of this inheritance is being kept for
us in heaven, and in the present life the heir sometimes
struggles on amid great need. But the will which makes him
an heir is signed with the very blood of the testator. His
inheritance is therefore not just a vague hope. He is from
now on a son, with all the rights, privileges and joyful duties
which this status gives him.

He is a son! Now who has ever managed to become a 'son'
by his own efforts, his own merits, his good behaviour, his
influence or his money? Who has ever been able to pro-
nounce himself the heir of one of this world's millionaires?
One only becomes an heir through the deliberate choice of
the testator. So, God himself has 'qualified us to share in the
inheritance of the saints in light' (NASB). 'To all who
received [Christ], to those who believed in his name, he gave
the right to become children of God — children born not of
natural descent, nor of human decision . . ., but born of God'
(John 1:12–13). 'It is by grace you have been saved' (Eph.

2:8). Humanly speaking, we had no right to this divine inheritance.

Neither, if we are honest, should we have known what to do with it! An inheritance can sometimes be a burden, even a hindrance. To know you are heir to a kingdom of holiness, purity and light, while preferring vice, sin and darkness, is not an exciting prospect! Most of the people we meet have not the least interest in what we call 'heaven'. They would be utterly miserable there. What a depressing inheritance it would be for them!

What a burden, too, Christianity can be for the non-Christian! How many young people, born into Christian families, have reluctantly been subjected to a form of godliness! What was a joy for the parents was merely a tiresome duty for the children.

But God has made us able 'to share [and share joyfully] in the inheritance of the saints in the kingdom of light' by giving us new birth. By making us his sons and daughters and creating in us a new nature with new inclinations, new affinities and new attitudes, he enables us to appreciate the light in which the saints enjoy fellowship together — and by 'saints' we mean those who, despite the sin still clinging to them, rejoice to be with God and love what is right, good, true and pure. The new nature that God has implanted in them thrives on these things, for it seeks the light.

This has already been *accomplished*: God has made them fit to take part in the inheritance which they will share with all the children of God in the kingdom of light. But it is also something which happens *progressively* and will come to completion on the day when the son takes full possession of all his Father's treasures.

It takes us a long time to learn how to appreciate our inheritance, and God is preparing us day by day, through the discipline of life and the teaching of his Word, for full enjoyment of our royal privileges. This distant prospect, however, should not make us neglect the glorious realities of the present.

Liberated

'He has rescued us from the dominion of darkness and brought us into the kingdom of the Son he loves.' This, too, is a present reality! Already we are in a different world, a different society: darkness has given way to light, tyranny to love; we who were slaves are now children of the King!

There is a big difference between what we are now and what we shall be one day, when this transitory life has passed away and eternal things have been revealed. But there is probably an even bigger difference between what we were before God intervened in our lives and what we are now. Perhaps we do not realize how wide a gulf we have bridged through God's grace, and the unbelieving world around may be even less aware of this change than we are. And yet we have really crossed over from one world into another. One day, in the perspective of eternity, we shall become aware of this extraordinary transition from death to life, and then our song of 'praise to the glory of God's grace' will take on new meaning.

'He has rescued us from the dominion of darkness and brought us into the kingdom of the Son he loves'! What a contrast! We were slaves and in darkness. Darkness is the state of separation from God and ignorance of him in which life, joy, suffering, striving and death have no meaning: there is total emptiness. We were slaves — in other words, we had no hope of escaping from this darkness, from the tyranny of sin which rules there. An irresistible force was continually dragging us down into this abyss of nothingness, and all our efforts to preserve our dignity only made us feel our bondage more keenly.

But the light has shone in the darkness! Jesus Christ has come down into this world of sin without the darkness entering his heart, without sin being able to enslave him. The Light has overcome the darkness, Holiness has conquered sin, and Life has come out of death. And this victory is our victory, for he won the battle on our behalf, in order to take us with him into his light.

He has freed us from an arbitrary and merciless tyranny to bring us into a kingdom — better still, to raise us to royal status! There is a world of difference between being a slave and belonging to a royal family. In the same way, there is a world of difference between the power of darkness and the kingdom of the Son of God, the kingdom of love, free self-giving and glad service. The rule of darkness meant servitude, revolt, impotence. The kingdom of the Son of God is the kingdom of freedom and love.

He has already brought us into it, for his reign began when, after his battle and his death, he was received into heaven to sit at his Father's right hand.

True, this kingdom is not yet visible in all its perfection and glory: sometimes it even seems to be smothered by the power of darkness, and yet it is here, 'among you', 'within you' (Luke 17:20,21). Though hidden, it is growing and no one can halt its progress: soon all the powers and kingdoms of the earth will give way before it. The King will appear and his kingdom will be established over all others.

Forgiven

'In whom we have redemption, the forgiveness of sins.' This is where it all begins — when we stop thinking that we are righteous or able to save ourselves and, instead, we accept the work that Jesus Christ came to do for us. Never in our own strength could we have escaped from the power of darkness: a slave has no way of obtaining his own freedom. But Jesus Christ has paid our ransom by giving his own life. Now the slave is free: 'In whom we have *redemption*'[1].

Also the crushing debt of sin which weighed us down is

---

[1] *Redemption* was the transaction by which a slave was 'bought back' so as to be set free.

cancelled. Never by all our good deeds, kind thoughts or sacrifices could we shake off this growing debt. Relentlessly, a
debit entry was brought forward to the head of each new
clean page of our lives. But now, in him 'we have *the forgiveness of sins*'. The debt is wiped out for ever, and in the great
book of life all the infinite wealth of the King of kings is
credited to our account! There is only one thing left for us to
do: joyfully give thanks to the Father.

6.
King of the universe

Please read Colossians 1:15–17

After catching sight of the kingdom, we are now brought into the presence of the King, 'the Son [God] loves', in whom we have inherited royal status and all the riches of God. We look away from the blessings to fix our gaze upon the one from whom they all come; our thoughts rise from the kingdom to the King himself.

It is not through historical or philosophical interpretation of Jesus Christ that our thoughts rise to him in this way, but through contemplation which leads us to worship him — first as Lord of the universe, then as Lord of the church.

Jesus Christ is Lord of the universe. We are now at the heart of Paul's argument against the false teachers who, while claiming to teach a better gospel, were dethroning Christ and assigning him a place among the many intermediaries which heretical thinkers had set up between God and man, and between God and the universe.

Christ and God

Christ is first shown to us in his relationship with God: '**He is the image of the invisible God**.' In him the 'invisible God' becomes visible; Christ is the manifestation and revelation of the Father.

It is true that man — the first Adam — was made in the image of God. But alas, in a mysterious way, sin entered the world and God's reflection in man was clouded and distorted; man let sin come between himself and God, and

God's light was no longer reflected in his heart. Since that
unhappy day, man has been left with only fragments of that
image; only a glimmer remains of that original brightness.

But Christ came, the second Adam, the perfect image of
God, the exact likeness of the Father. This image was not
just a copy, for in Christ God revealed *himself*: 'God was
pleased to have all his fulness dwell in him' (1:19). And Paul
makes the same idea clear later in this epistle: 'In Christ all
the fulness of the Deity lives in bodily form' (2:9). Again
when writing to the Corinthians he says, 'God was in Christ
reconciling the world to himself' (2 Cor. 5:19, NASB). Also,
the apostle John tells us that no one has seen God and that
only Christ has made him known to us (John 1:18). He has
shown him to us in the way a son looks like his father. Jesus
himself says, 'Anyone who has seen me has seen the Father'
(John 14:9).

God cannot be known apart from Jesus Christ, and any
who think they do not need Jesus in order to know and worship God are greatly mistaken. Any god other than the God
who reveals himself in Jesus Christ is a figment of human
imagination or emotions, a god in the image of man, the
reflection of man's ideals and man's weaknesses. No knowledge of God is possible apart from Jesus of Nazareth, born
in Bethlehem, crucified on Golgotha, risen from the dead and
raised to glory — that is, the Jesus of the Scriptures.

So all those today who have reduced Jesus to the level of a
mere man, even though he were the greatest of men, or to a
mere prophet, even the greatest of prophets, have lost the
basic idea about God and will never be able to know him.
Without Christ, God remains unknown and no 'theology' is
possible.

Christ and the universe

Just as we cannot know God without Christ, so the universe,

too, is beyond our understanding without him. '**He is ... the first-born over all creation. For by him all things were created: things in heaven and on earth ... all things were created by him and for him. He is before all things, and in him all things hold together**.'

The title *'first-born over all creation'* could be misunderstood. The Colossians certainly understood it aright in their particular circumstances and in the context of the heresy which was troubling them, but it needs clarifying for us. It does not mean, as might be supposed, that Christ is part of creation, the first being that God created. Paul's thinking is precisely the opposite: his aim is to show that Christ is not one of the many intermediaries which God was supposed to have created and placed between himself and man, for not only was Christ not created, but he is the Creator.

He is before, after and over all things: this is in fact what the title 'first-born over all creation' means. 'The first-born' does not only mean the one who was born first (this meaning does not apply to Christ), but also the *heir*, to whom authority belongs. Christ is not first in time, but first in authority. He is over all things. This meaning is brought out in the psalm: 'I will also appoint him my firstborn, the most exalted of the kings of the earth' (Psalm 89:27).

Christ is Master and Lord of the universe, because he is its beginning and its end, the Alpha and the Omega, its origin and its goal, and all that links the one with the other.

It is he who created *'all ... things in heaven'*: the vast multitude of the stars, all the amazing energy which men are gradually discovering and which could be so frightening in their hands. Only God, who created it, can control this incredible power. Without Jesus Christ or apart from him, this universe, endowed with order and power and created in wisdom, loses all meaning and stability.

It is he who created *'all ... things on earth'*, in particular life, that impenetrable mystery which is as wonderful as the universe itself and is built on the same model, possesses the same structure and is moved by the same forces and the same amazing power — Christ, the Lord of life. Between the things in heaven and those on earth a perfect unity is apparent, proclaiming their divine origin. Apart from Jesus Christ this living world is incomprehensible. Many people try to explain its origin without the 'hypothesis of God', but they have not yet managed to formulate a valid and satisfactory theory. When we try to leave out God and Jesus Christ in explaining the world, it loses all its meaning and becomes a vast insoluble riddle.

Again it is he who created *'all things . . . visible and invisible'* — the material world and the spiritual world. In this connection Paul immediately lists some of those unseen things to which the false teachers of Colosse evidently attached great importance: *'thrones,   powers,   rulers,   authorities'*.   The Jews had divided heaven into different zones and set up a whole hierarchy of spiritual powers. Paganism, too, had its religious systems and superstitions (2:8–10, 15). Paul only touches on these controversies in order to declare that, even if these unseen powers have any reality, Jesus Christ cannot be put on a par with them. He is above them all.

He is not only the Creator, but the one *in whom 'all things hold together'*. He did not leave the world to itself after creating it; he is still in charge. Even though, through permission mysteriously granted by God, Satan still holds his usurped power, Jesus Christ remains in control of world events. The mystery of evil is certainly at work, but only the mystery of grace can unlock the true meaning of the history of the nations and of individuals. We can see this intermingling of evil and grace in Christ's very death (Acts 2:23, 24). The Lord was indeed to suffer death — that masterpiece of the power of evil — and yet far from being a victory for evil his death was to prove a victory for love, for on the cross Jesus *gave* his life; no one *took* it from him (John 10:18). And so, in the history of nations and individuals, grace has turned defeats into victories, downfall into deliverance, curses into blessings, and trials into sources of joy (e.g. Gen. 45:7, 8; 50:20; Rom. 8:28; John 19:11).

Finally, Jesus Christ stands at the end of this world. He is the final purpose in which all the powers of the universe and all the events of history are brought together. '*All things were created . . . for him.*' It is impossible to explain either the future or the past, the end or the beginning of the universe or of man, apart from Jesus Christ.

Some philosophers think that the world is being irresistibly carried along by progress and advancing towards the deification of man, that the forces governing the world are converging on that one distant point. But the Word of God, which also speaks of this convergence, teaches that this point, this light, is not man deified, but Jesus Christ, the one who brings together the transient and the eternal, the human and the divine, man and God.

The end of the world *is* Jesus Christ, his coming again, and the establishment of a new world and a new humanity. Without this hope there is nothing but despair, emptiness and death. Only when we really understand this will our own lives become meaningful. The universe is the realization of God's great master-plan which, has its origin, its focus and its fulfilment in Jesus Christ. When we have bowed the knee before him, then this world will become intelligible and hope will bring a new light to our life and history. When we have joyfully entered into this plan of God's, the tensions of life will melt away and peace will flood our hearts.

He is the Lord of creation, the Master of the universe, the King of our souls. Therefore let us take courage: our life is in his hands. We have nothing to fear. He is the *Lord*. Let us bow down and worship him.

7.
The Head of the church

Please read Colossians 1:18–20

Christ, Lord of the universe, is also the Head of the church. The 'firstborn over all creation', that is, the Lord of every created thing, is also the **'firstborn from among the dead'**, that is, the Head of the new humanity, the church. As Creator, he takes first place in the universe, and as Redeemer he takes first place in the church. Thus he has 'the supremacy *in everything'*.

All things are gathered into one in Christ, and in him the world finds perfect unity. In thus affirming the universal primacy of Christ, Paul is already countering the error which threatened the Colossians and has attracted many other Christians throughout history right up to the present day: namely, that of thinking that the world is divided between two opposing powers — God and Satan; good and evil — and that goodness resides in the spirit while evil is inherent in matter, in the 'flesh' (2:23).

Christ, who is the author, the principle and the goal of all things, is the source of harmony; in him all conflict is resolved. Thus the first creation recovers its meaning and its fulness — and man his freedom — in the second creation. For through him God chose **'to reconcile to himself all things, whether things on earth or things in heaven, by making peace through his blood, shed on the cross'**.

Christ, King of the universe, is the Head of the church, the new creation, the new society, which he founded by his resurrection from the dead. What he is and what he has done for the church are good reasons for us to worship him.

The Head of the church

'**He is the head of the body, the church**.' This is true of the universal church, the church as the Bride of Christ, but it must also be true of the local church. The apostle's assertion must be the basis and aim of all that is done within the community of Christian brothers and sisters. Christ must 'have first place in everything' (NASB).

Authority within the church is not vested in a pontiff, a hierarchy, a synod, a pastor, elders or the members in general. The Head of the church is and must be Jesus Christ alone; not just in theory but in actual fact. No doubt it is difficult for us to put this into practice, yet if we do not, there is no real church.

The church is not simply a human organization — though, of course, it is that, since it is composed of people with their limitations and shortcomings. It is divine in origin: it is the body of Jesus Christ, and he as Lord must be allowed to exercise his full authority over it and in it. It is not for one man or several, nor even for the members as a whole, to rule it. Whatever structures and types of government it may adopt in different times and places, these can have no value or meaning except in so far as they serve and give expression to the authority of its Lord: Christ must reign.

We have no authority to make rules, either individually or collectively. Our job as members of the body is to discern the will of Christ its Head, whether his will appeals to us or not, whether it increases or reduces our numbers, whether it makes us popular or unpopular, whether it brings us the praise or the scorn of men. If the church is to be obedient to Christ, its Head, each of its members must be obedient to him *personally*, for it is only as each member obeys the Master and the teaching of the gospel (Rom. 6:17) — not the rule of a church or of an individual — that the unity of the body will become a reality.

The submission of the Christian to the church and to the shepherds of the flock is always subject to obedience to Jesus Christ. The respect, love and loyalty which he owes them do not mean that the Christian should submit to them blindly or against his conscience (1 Thess. 5:12). Indeed, this submission can only be thought of as 'in the Lord', that is, when the authority of the church elders is exercised in line with the word and spirit of our Lawgiver, the Head of the church. So, however a church is organized, it should aim to guide every Christian to Christ himself (John 3:28–30); and it would be dangerous to encourage him to be loyal to the church rather than to Christ, to expect him to obey men rather than his Lord. Certainly, love for the church and obedience to its leaders normally go hand in hand with devotion to Christ (2 Cor. 8:5); but it is important not to confuse cause and effect. The church has suffered greatly from the hypocrisy, intolerance and persecution which this kind of muddled thinking has caused. Christ is and remains the only Head of the church, and that means the only Head of each church member.

Such a principle clearly has its risks and may leave the door wide open to anarchy within the church and to certain dangerous aberrations. But here we are touching on the problem of individual freedom. Who would think of abolishing freedom on the pretext that most people do not know how to use it? Things would be far worse!

Christ must reign! This should be the aim of all organization and all rules. The local church should constantly seek to let Christ be seen, to let Christ be heard, to point the way to obedience to Christ according to his Word; if it does not do so, it is in danger of losing its calling and being no more than a human organization.

'Christ is the head of the body, the church.' This spiritual truth must become a tangible, living reality, so that he may 'have first place in everything'.

The grounds of his authority

Paul now lists the reasons why Christ has the right to this supreme authority in the church: his deity, his resurrection and his work of redemption.

First, his *deity*: '**God was pleased to have all his fulness dwell in him**', or as Paul says later, 'In Christ all the fulness of the Deity lives in bodily form' (2:9).

This brings us to the very heart of Christianity. Jesus Christ is God in his fulness; a partly hidden God[1], certainly, whom we can only discern through faith and with the help of divine enlightenment (Matt. 16:17), but nevertheless God in the fulness of his person, in his infinity and his eternity.

In his incarnation, Jesus did not submit passively to human limitations, but he took them on himself of his own free will. When in a mysterious way he restricted himself to the physical and psychological capabilities of a man (Luke 2:40; Matt. 24:36), he was making full and conscious use of his divine faculties. For his authority over creation and over his own death (John 10:18) reminds us that even within these human limitations he was still in possession of his freedom and his divine powers. All the fulness of God dwells in Jesus Christ permanently, eternally. There was not a moment, even in his greatest humiliation, when he was not fully God.

Thus Jesus Christ is not simply the founder of a religion or a spiritual teacher. He is truly God made manifest in human form. That is why we can worship him (John 20:28) and acknowledge him as the only head of the church. That is why we accept his teachings without question and do not venture to alter, add to or take away from them in any way.

[1] As the rays of the sun would destroy all life here on earth if they were not filtered, so the direct brilliance of God would instantly consume sinful man. The 'radiance of God's glory' (Heb. 1:3), the revelation of the perfect nature of the divine attributes which took on human form in Christ, this we can look upon, but not God's 'face': 'You cannot see my face, for no one may see me and live' (Exodus 33:20). It is therefore through the veil of Christ's flesh that man sees God (John 1:14, 18; 14:9).

Secondly, we shall consider his *resurrection*: '**He is the first-born from among the dead**.' He is the Head of all who will rise from the dead, he is pre-eminent among them; but he is also the first in time to have risen, and in this sense Christ is not only the cause but also the guarantor and pattern of the resurrection of all those who are yet to be raised.

Lazarus and the few others who came back to life did not rise in the same way as Jesus rose. For them it was resuscitation rather than resurrection in the true sense of the word. No doubt they regained the life they had lost, but it was the same life; and although their days on earth were prolonged, they did not escape death for all that. They did not live for ever, they had to die again. Jesus rose to die no more: 'For we know that since Christ was raised from the dead, he cannot die again' (Rom. 6:9). Jesus himself said, 'I am the First and the Last. I am the *Living One*; I was dead, and behold I am alive for ever and ever!' (Rev. 1:18.)

On Easter morning he appeared in a new body, alive with a new life. All the redeemed will share in this immortality (1 Cor. 15:36–38, 42–44). Christ's resurrection is the guarantee of our own (1 Cor. 15:12–20), for he is the firstborn from among the dead, the first of a countless posterity.

Finally, Christ's third title to sovereignty is his *love* as it is revealed in his work of redemption. '**God was pleased ... through him to reconcile to himself all things, whether things on earth or things in heaven, by making peace through his blood, shed on the cross**.' Is that not his best claim to our gratitude, and so to our obedience? Since he has brought us back to God, reconciled us to God by his sacrifice on the cross, is he not entitled to our love and adoration?

Previously we belonged to Christ as a creature belongs to its Creator, for we were created *by* him and *for* him. But through our redemption we belong to him twice over, for God also chose to reconcile all things *by* him and *for* him.

'God was pleased ... to reconcile to himself *all things*'. What does Paul mean by 'all things, whether things on earth or things in heaven'? There is knowing talk these days about the 'cosmic dimension of salvation'. This idea may be present here, but Paul does not enlarge on it at all. He goes straight to the earthly and human dimensions of the reconciliation accomplished by Christ (1:21, 22). His aim is not to lead us into speculation but to adoration; that is why he focuses our attention on one specific place on the earth at a single moment in history: he shows us the cross. There the Lord of the universe died to reconcile us to his Father, *our* Father.

God had made us for himself, to give him joy, but we preferred to please ourselves rather than please him. He had made us for light, but we preferred darkness. Sin broke all relations between him and us: he remained in the light, but our fall plunged us into darkness. We deliberately wrecked everything, thinking this was how to live and be free, but then we found we were alone, slaves in the night, amid the ruins we had made, with all hope gone. This is what we deserved, and we alone brought it on ourselves.

But God, in his wonderful mercy, did not leave us to our rightful fate. With all his heart and with all his power he chose to reconcile us to himself, to bring us back into harmony with himself; and he, who had never stopped loving us and had nothing to do with our folly, consented to pay its appalling price—the death of his Son on the cross.

If it is true that the power and authority of God constrain us, it is also true that 'Christ's love compels us, because we are convinced that one died for all, and therefore all died. And he died for all, that those who live should no longer live for themselves but for him who died for them and was raised again' (2 Cor. 5:14,15).

8.
Man's salvation

Please read Colossians 1:21–23

Sin has destroyed God's harmonious order. Since the rift in Eden, creation has been in disarray and 'groaning' for deliverance (Rom. 8:19–22). The human race, too, by breaking away from God, has lost everything: it has sunk into a dark and empty existence. Man can see no sense in life; he has lost his way in a world he cannot understand and both he and it are heading for inevitable death.

But God has not abandoned the universe or mankind to their fate. Throughout the ages since man first broke away, God has 'made known to us the mystery of his will according to his good pleasure, which he purposed in Christ, ... to bring all things in heaven and on earth together under one head, even Christ' (Eph. 1:9, 10). It is in the incarnation or, more precisely, at the cross, that God 'recapitulates' so to speak, makes a fresh start and brings all things back into a harmonious new creation of which Christ is the head—the beginning, the source of life and the Lord.

It would, however, be dangerous to content ourselves with admiring this work of God—which Paul describes so impressively—and not to enter into it personally. For this reason the apostle refuses to wander off into the infinity of the universe or human thought. He keeps firmly before him men's practical, immediate and individual needs. It is on this level that he meets with us as we face our personal problems, and we shall see how perfectly the gospel of Jesus Christ meets the problems of our world today and the needs of man throughout all time.

Past alienation

'**Once you were alienated**.' Paul's words have a very modern ring about them. They correspond to certain feelings which are very widespread in our day, feelings of not belonging, of alienation (in the modern sense of the term[1]).

Young people, for example, feel out of place in the society built by the older generation, and older people feel the same way towards the young. Workers have a 'them-and-us' attitude towards management; employers are out of touch with their employees; there is a mutual absence of understanding, for everyone lives in a world of his own.

Dissatisfaction gnaws at the heart of man, even though in many ways he has all he could wish for. Having tried everything, he is still hungry. He feels that no one understands him, that he is alone in an empty world, lost in a meaningless universe. Furthermore, he finds he is the victim of a society into which he is slowly being absorbed, and the plaything of forces which hold him captive, however strongly he resists.

Young people, who are possibly less insensitive and less resigned to this alienation than their elders, may quite understandably adopt an attitude of questioning and revolt. They are thus rebelling against the emptiness of life, against enslavement to the implacable idols of the day — and this is a healthy reaction which shows that some humanity, some human dignity remains, even if those alienating powers are not always identified correctly.

The worst mistake would be to suppose that this alienation, experienced by young and old alike, is simply something one undergoes, something passive. '**You were**,' says the apostle, '**enemies in your minds because of your evil behaviour**.' Estrangement has become aggressiveness and enmity.

---

[1] 'Condition of the individual who, as a result of outward circumstances (economic, political, religious), is no longer his own master, is treated as an object, and becomes the slave of material things and of man's very achievements which turn against him' (trans. from *Dictionnaire Robert*).

Anyone who has not discovered anew in God the meaning of life, who has not found peace in Christ, is a rebel against God. He is not only a stranger to God, to his thoughts, his purpose and his providence; he actually becomes an enemy of God. Lack of understanding leads to revolt. And the person who is at war with God is also at war with others and with himself. He has no peace, and for this he blames all the world: parents, young people, authority, employers, workers, wife or husband, friends or competitors, society or God — everyone except himself. That, however, is where the problem lies — in ourselves. That is where the Bible locates it, and where it seeks to apply the remedy.

Present reconciliation

'**Now he has reconciled you**.' Peace has now been restored — peace with ourselves and peace with others, through our reconciliation to God in Christ.

The deep cause of man's revolt — a cause of which he is unaware, or which he rules out, or else will not admit — is sin: it is sin which prevents any close bond between man and God, and obscures the meaning of life.

Life cannot be thought of apart from God; if God is not its foundation, its centre and its goal, man wanders aimlessly, he no longer has any guiding principle, he is literally 'lost'. If he is to regain unity and harmony within himself and with other people, he must regain unity and harmony with God. This can only happen if sin, which separates us from God, is taken away.

'Now *he* has reconciled you.' That is God's great work! It can only be his. Who can blot out sin, or forgive the sinner? Certainly not the sinner himself! Only the offended party, God, has the right to do that. Time cannot wipe out the sins we have committed, nor can our good deeds make up for them. Neither goodwill, nor wealth, nor tears, nor sacrifices can ever bring back to life someone who has been killed, or recall lying gossip once it is spoken, or retrieve a wasted life! No, not even our noblest deeds can restore to life the one whom we crucified by our sin. But now he has reconciled us, paying himself the incalculable price for our sin!

'**He has reconciled you by Christ's physical body through death**', by a real body of flesh and blood, like our own, in which he came to die for us.

Once man is reconciled with God, he discovers what life is all about. The world, which before was so alien to him, takes on a new meaning; he sees the people around him in a completely new light and all hostility towards them vanishes. In finding God he finds others and he finds himself. He discovers a new harmony; he is at peace!

This does not mean, however, that all his problems are solved. The harmony enjoyed by the child of God is still relative, since at the moment he lives in a world at enmity with God. And the world carries its warfare into the Christian's heart. So his joy is mingled with tears and his peace with suffering. Paul himself, who exhorted everyone to be joyful (Phil. 3:1), wept in anguish over the sufferings of others and over the contradictions in his own life (Rom. 9:2; 7:13–25).

Future perfection

The absolute and final victory is not of this world, but it is coming. For if Christ has reconciled us, it is '**to present [us] holy in his sight, without blemish and free from accusation**'. He who began this work of peace will carry it on to completion as he has promised (Phil. 1:6). He has pledged his word and he will not leave the work unfinished. His honour is at stake. At present, the results of the completed work of the cross are still incomplete and relative (1 Cor. 15:27, 28, 54; 2 Cor. 4:16–5:7), but one day they will appear in all their perfection. Peace, so often marred by tears today, will then shine on every face, in every heart, and in a world which has been reconciled.

'The creation waits in eager expectation for the sons of God to be revealed. For the creation was subjected to frustration . . . in hope that the creation itself will be liberated from its bondage to decay and brought into the glorious freedom of the children of God. We know that the whole creation has been groaning as in the pains of childbirth right up to the present time. Not only so, but we ourselves, who have the firstfruits of the Spirit, groan inwardly as we wait eagerly for our adoption as sons, the redemption of our bodies. For in this hope we were saved' (Rom. 8:19–24). This hope is firm and secure (Heb. 6:18, 19; 1 Peter 1:3–5). One day, we shall be perfectly 'holy, without blemish and free from accusation' when Christ presents us before God, even though he is the most strict, scrupulous and just of all judges.

How we long to serve God without grieving him, to fulfil his expectations, to gladden his heart! That is what 'heaven' is! Then there will be no more sorrow or weeping, and the child of God will experience in unending peace the full extent of Christ's reconciling work.

But we must come down to earth — Paul leaves us in no doubt of that — for the perfection we have been speaking of is still in the realm of hope. Having once been outsiders and enemies, we are now reconciled, and one day we shall appear before God in all perfection. Yet we have to remember that, although this refining process is the work of God, it will not be carried out without our co-operation, it will not just happen as if by magic on the last day. Between present reconciliation and future perfection God is constantly at work in us, preparing us for glory. There is no doubt that it is *his* work, but it is carried out in us and through us, through our perseverance, in faith and in hope. The condition, says the apostle, is that '**you continue in your faith, established and firm, not moved from the hope held out in the gospel. This is the gospel that you heard and that has been**

proclaimed to every creature under heaven, and of which I, Paul, have become a servant.'

God himself promises to fulfil this condition, but he will not fulfil it in spite of us, without asking for our consent and our efforts. He will fulfil it by setting our wills to work and stirring us into action (Phil. 2:13). It will not come about without battles, failures and tears; yet it will not be our own strength at work, but the power of God himself displayed in our weakness (Col. 1:29; Phil. 4:13).

The Lord of the universe is also the Lord of our lives. We are the clay; he is the divine potter and can fashion us into vessels of beauty which one day will bring glory to him in his eternal kingdom!

This is the gospel of Jesus Christ, of which Paul was a servant, 'the gospel ... that has been proclaimed to every creature under heaven' so as to bring us peace when we are alienated, torn asunder by strife and doomed to die. Who could disregard so great a salvation or ignore such a generous offer of peace?

9.
Paul, the servant of the church

Please read Colossians 1:24–29

Paul, the servant of Jesus Christ and the servant of the gospel, is also the servant of the church. When he gave himself to Jesus Christ, he also gave himself to the church which is his body. He is not the head of the church, nor is he one head among others, for the church acknowledges no head but Christ, but he is its servant; it is not for him to rule the church, but to teach it by proclaiming the gospel in all its glory and with all its demands. This is a hard and sometimes painful task!

In this passage, the apostle gives a brief glimpse of the battle he is fighting in his own life. He tells us of the sufferings he endures in carrying out his task, of the glorious message he bears, and finally of the purpose of his ministry.

His sufferings

'**Now I rejoice in my sufferings for your sake, and in my flesh I do my share on behalf of his body (which is the church) in filling up that which is lacking in Christ's afflictions. Of this church I was made a minister according to the stewardship from God bestowed on me for your benefit**' (NASB). These words may seem strange. Some may see in them a morbid interest in suffering for its own sake. This would be to misunderstand Paul's character. He never went looking for hardships; what he did was to submit to them and bear them as being an integral part of his ministry.

But at the thought of Christ's wonderful work of reconciliation, of which he has already spoken, at the thought of all God's love which he has come to proclaim to a lost world, he cannot help rejoicing in his sufferings. 'Yes', he seems to say, in spite of my weakness, my sin, my persecution of the church, God has granted to me, Paul, the privilege of continuing the work of Christ, of sharing and even completing his sufferings.'

It is most important to understand which of Christ's sufferings are meant here, for they are not all of the same kind and a distinction must be made. On one hand, there is the agony on the cross which led up to his redeeming death. On the other hand, there are the sufferings which accompanied his earthly ministry: the physical and psychological distress which is the lot of anyone who defends the truth or condemns the injustices and sins of the world. Thus he suffered hunger, thirst and lack of sleep, but he was hurt most of all by the unbelief of Jerusalem, at which he wept tears of sorrow, by the trying lack of understanding of his own disciples and friends and by the heartbreaking treachery of Judas.

The former — Christ's sufferings in his work of atonement and redemption — are absolutely unique. No man could share them, and in this sense when our Lord died, all was finished and complete (John 19:30). Nothing could be added to his sufferings: his sacrifice was perfect. The latter, on the other hand — the afflictions linked with his ministry — were not over; the Master's faithful disciples could, and in fact did, share them. James, Stephen and Paul himself were each in their turn to undergo many trials and finally to give their lives for the gospel. Those sufferings, endured for the sake of the church, are surely the continuation and complement of Christ's sufferings (2 Cor. 11:23–29), and all who, like Paul, love the church, the body of Christ, will experience Paul's sufferings, which were also the sufferings of Christ.

Love, the source of the greatest joy, is also the cause of the greatest suffering. He who loves little, suffers little. Anyone who does not love the church does not feel pain at the blemishes which mar it, or the failings and sins which discredit it, thus marring and discrediting its Head, Jesus Christ himself.

Anyone who does not love Christ cannot love his body, the church, but conversely, anyone who does not love the church does not love Christ, its Head, for the two are inseparable: the *Lord*, who is perfect, eternally pure and holy, and the *church*, which is imperfect and stained with the sins of its members.

One day this body will appear in the perfect beauty which it has been promised (Eph. 5:27; Rev. 21:2), but until that great and glorious day the true servants of Jesus Christ, the true disciples of the Lord, will struggle and suffer. Paul, writing to the Galatians, says, 'My dear children, for whom I am again in the pains of childbirth until Christ is formed in you' (Gal. 4:19). This suffering is not in vain, it carries within itself its own reward and joy, for it is the pain of childbirth and leads to life, to a new world, to Christ.

His message

But what is the message for which the apostle is ready to go through all this suffering and to give his life? '**The Word of God in its fulness — the mystery that has been kept hidden for ages and generations, but is now disclosed to the saints. To them God has chosen to make known among the Gentiles the glorious riches of this mystery, which is Christ in you, the hope of glory.**'

The gospel is here presented as a 'mystery', and the Colossians could not fail to connect this in their minds with the pagan mysteries. Certain cults of the time — and probably the ones which were influencing religious life in Colosse — were related to the mystery religions. The 'mysteries' were symbolic rites which allegedly gave an explanation for the

origin of life, for sin, and for the happiness or doom awaiting
man after death. Paul, on his way from Athens to Corinth,
went through the town of Eleusis, which was famous for the
mysterious rites performed there. In a huge temple a special
elite, the 'perfect ones', were initiated into secret doctrines.
There can be little doubt that Paul is using the words 'mystery' and 'perfect' intentionally. They belong to the mystical
vocabulary of those Colossians who thought they were
enriching Christianity by adding to it certain doctrines and
rituals from pagan mysticism.

But what a difference between the 'mystery' of the gospel
and the mysteries of paganism! There is nothing secret about
the gospel: 'it is now disclosed' to all who receive it out of
love for the truth; it is *made known* to the ends of the earth.
Far from being a secret, unintelligible teaching reserved for
the initiated few, it is addressed to 'everyone', a point which
Paul is at pains to stress[1]. Worked out over the centuries by a
God of love, grace and wisdom, the 'mystery' of the gospel is
now accessible to us all. We do not have to be specially
clever to understand it, nor do we have to be wealthy to
obtain it; childlike simplicity is enough to grasp it, and the
heart which knows its own need can receive it, thanks to the
light of the Spirit.

This 'mystery' did not remain the privilege of one nation,
the Jews; it was proclaimed to the Gentiles, it came to find
them, it was revealed among them. It is not a doctrine, nor
rituals, but a person: *Jesus Christ*. Perhaps this great truth
would stand out even more clearly if one translated more
literally: 'the wealth of the *glory* of this mystery'. The 'glory',
in Old Testament language, is nothing less than the 'glory of
God', the visible manifestation of his presence; and that, for
us today, is Jesus Christ himself. This glory, which was the
privilege of Israel, is not only revealed but is present today
among all nations. As they share in Christ by union with
him, they will one day share in this glory.

---

[1] 'Everyone' occurs three times in the Greek of v. 28.

His purpose

'**Christ . . . the hope of glory**': it is *him* we proclaim, repeats
Paul, before explaining the purpose of what he is doing for
the church. '**Admonishing and teaching everyone**.' These
two complementary aspects of his ministry may become
clearer if we compare them with similar words he used when
talking to the elders of the Ephesus church: 'I have
declared . . . that they must turn to God in *repentance* and
have *faith* in our Lord Jesus' (Acts 20:21).

There is no salvation without repentance; nor is there any
progress in the Christian life without repentance. Repentance
is not only for someone coming to God for the first time. It is
both the Christian's duty and the grace offered to him during
the whole of his life in Christ. 'If we claim to be without sin,
we deceive ourselves and the truth is not in us . . . if we claim
we have not sinned, we make [God] out to be a liar' (1 John
1:8, 10). So it is part of the mission of God's servants to
condemn sin and error and to preach repentance — a difficult and thankless task, but absolutely essential. Long ago
God spoke solemnly to Ezekiel: 'When . . . you do not warn
[the wicked man] or speak out to dissuade him from his evil
ways in order to save his life, that wicked man will die in his
sin, and I will hold you accountable for his blood' (Ezekiel
3:18). Echoing these words, Paul writes, 'Woe to me if I do
not preach the gospel!' (1 Cor. 9:16.)

It is also the apostle's job to teach, to build on the ground
cleared beforehand by repentance, to build up the Christian
in his faith. Let us remember that the Christian life begins
with knowledge, and the quality of this life depends on a
constantly renewed knowledge of Christ and his Word (Col.
1:9, 10). True knowledge will generate true faith and make it
grow, and such faith will not fail to bear fruit in the Christian's life. Unproductive faith, which does not express itself
in deeds, is dead! (James 2:26.)

'**Teaching everyone with all wisdom**.' Paul is not trying

to produce a blind faith. God never asks for a fanciful or superstitious faith, or one that is not properly thought out. The gospel itself is 'wisdom' (1 Cor. 2:6). Though faith is based on the unseen, that does not mean it is blind; trust in God, from its beginning and throughout its growth, comes from knowing him in our heart and mind. It is this continually growing knowledge that will enable the Christian to develop from a child into a man. For salvation has not stopped at our conversion: in God it is already perfect, but in us it is a continuing process, and Paul's aim is nothing less than to 'present everyone perfect in Christ'.

The 'perfect one', in pagan religions, was the initiate, the privileged one, superior to others; but also, in a wider sense, the mature adult as opposed to the child. Paul probably understands it in the latter sense and longs to be able to apply it to all Christians. All Jesus Christ's new people form an 'aristocracy', and paradoxically there is no other social class among them! All the members who make up the church, even though at different stages in their spiritual development, are kings and priests for God (Rev. 1:6).

This brings us back to Paul's insistence on the collective aspect of this perfection: he admonishes 'everyone' and teaches 'everyone' in order to bring 'everyone' to this spiritual maturity. His aim is not to foster an elite within the church; he is not interested in spurring a few of the abler members towards heights of attainment while neglecting the rest of the flock. His aim is to nurture and train the whole family of God so that all will progress towards spiritual maturity; and this the Spirit will use to ensure that the church survives and maintains a faithful witness in the world.

This is the great ambition which fills Paul as he faces the pain and suffering of spiritual childbirth (2 Cor. 4:7–12; 12:14, 15). '**To this end I labour, struggling with all his energy, which so powerfully works in me**.'

Have we who are children of God realized the full extent of

the glorious riches of the gospel, and are we then, like Paul, aiming at this perfection in Christ? Do we care for others enough to correct them in love and teach them in wisdom until they become fully mature in Christ? Do we love the church — and not just our own local fellowship — enough to be willing to suffer for her until she appears without any stain or wrinkle before her heavenly Bridegroom?   If so, we too shall know something of the sufferings and joys of Christ, something of the riches of the gospel, the hope of glory!

10.
Doing battle for the church

Please read Colossians 2:1–7

Like every church which is alive, the one at Colosse had its problems, and Paul, like every pastor who loves his Lord, suffered for the church which is Christ's body. The church will have times of sickness and its servants will undergo suffering: both are inevitable in this life and both are bound up together.

Having looked at Paul's sufferings for the church as a whole, we now come to the particular *battle* for God which he waged in the church at Colosse. '**I want you to know how much I am struggling for you and for those at Laodicea, and for all who have not met me personally.**'

The Colossians and their brothers in Laodicea were in danger. True, the gospel was revered among them: it was bearing fruit; the faith of most of them was healthy, and their love for each other was real and practical. But they seemed to be hankering after something new. Perhaps they were a little tired of their daily fare. Possibly they felt tempted to look elsewhere for other experiences, other thrills and doctrines of 'greater depth' which false teachers were ready to promise or teach them. '**I tell you this so that no one may deceive you by fine-sounding arguments.**'

In all ages, various movements or sects have been on the look-out for the dissatisfied people to be found in all churches, offering them formulae for deepening their spiritual lives or more advanced teaching. They do not hesitate to claim that by reading their books, attending their lectures and accepting their teaching, everyone can acquire more comprehensive knowledge, superior knowledge, which will provide the key to all problems — those of the individual and those of the world. The obvious imperfection of the churches makes it the more likely that such arguments will gain a favourable hearing.

The craving for the novel, the original and the mysterious which was apparently gaining ground in the Colossian church, and the unsettling effect this was having, disturbed the apostle all the more since he was a long way off and had never met its members. That is why, on the one hand, he wrestles in *prayer* and, on the other, *warns* the Colossian Christians by means of this letter. In it he aims first to influence the atmosphere within the church and the character of its members. Then he goes on to remind them of the all-sufficiency of Christ; as we know, this is the central theme of his message.

The atmosphere within the church

First, Paul uses an indirect approach and deals with the atmosphere within the church. The two determining factors in a bacterial disease are the presence of bacteria and the general condition of the patient. So any treatment aims not only at fighting the bacteria but also at improving the general health. When this is deficient, the disease can more easily gain a foothold. The same applies in the spiritual sphere. When the Christian or the church is in poor general health, there is a fertile breeding-ground for heresies. Paul realizes that one of the factors causing a hunger for novelty is dissatisfaction. That is why he prays earnestly that the Colossians '**may be encouraged in heart**'.

Sadness, sorrow and worry, which are forms of dissatisfaction, often explain the search for novelty or for wonder remedies. For example, anxiety about the dead leads some people to seek contact with them through the occult. King Saul, filled with fear, resorted to this practice to try to obtain what God was withholding from him (1 Sam. 28:5–25). Similarly, some people today, finding that Christianity does not meet their needs, seek an answer to their anguish in this or that misguided sect. Others, who in sickness are unable to find peace in the comforting presence of their heavenly Friend, seek a more radical solution by turning to those who specialize in divine healing. Christ is not enough for them, they also insist on healing of the body, or some other material or even 'spiritual' benefit.

'**That their hearts may be filled with encouragement**', with the protecting peace of God (Phil. 4:7) — that is the apostle's wish in his concern for his readers' spiritual well-being. Anxiety and fear are bad counsellors. They attract false comforters and false consolations which can lead to dangerous errors.

Divisions in the church also open the door to error. That is why Paul wrestles in prayer that the Colossians may be '**united in love**'. Unity in love, that love 'which binds . . . all together in perfect unity', is one of the best antidotes to error.

Elsewhere Paul writes, 'Make my joy complete by being likeminded, having the same love, being one in spirit and purpose' (Phil. 2:2). And he adds in the negative, 'Do nothing out of selfish ambition.' When we form exclusive groups we begin to go wrong. One finds certain 'super-spiritual' Christians who are ready to split the church because by their standards some of their brothers are not spiritual or holy enough. If they are in the majority they shut out the 'unworthy' ones; if they are in the minority, they have no hesitation in leaving their brothers in order to fulfil their aspirations elsewhere, in 'more spiritual' company. 'In humility consider others better than yourselves. Each of you should look not only to your own interests, but also to the interests of others. Your attitude should be the same as that of Christ Jesus' (Phil. 2:3–5). This is the secret of unity, a powerful bulwark against error.

Lack of spiritual discernment is clearly a third reason why people go astray into error. That is why Paul works and struggles for the Colossians, praying that they '**may have the full riches of complete understanding**'.

Loving does not mean accepting everything so as to offend no one. The unity the apostle is thinking of is not a blind unity achieved regardless of the cost. It is a clear-sighted, perceptive unity, respecting and based upon the truth.

In the spiritual realm, discernment has never been more necessary than today, and we should take to heart John's warning: 'Do not believe every spirit, but test the spirits to see whether they are from God, because many false prophets have gone out into the world' (1 John 4:1). Christianity is weakened whenever the church, in the name of so-called love, does not discern error, does not condemn it unequivocally, or does not boldly dissociate itself from it.

Taking up the last phrase of our passage, '**overflowing with thankfulness**', can we not add that gratitude and praise are also a valuable guard against error? Surely being ungrateful, or always demanding more, are part of a fundamental error: they show lack of appreciation of the real cost of grace, salvation and truth. That is how they become sources of error. On the other hand, awareness of the infinite value of these gifts of God, and sincere, well-informed and constantly renewed gratitude will keep the Christian in the light of Christ. So instead of grumbling, be 'overflowing with thankfulness'! Make sure you are!

It is in such a climate of encouragement, unity, discernment and thankfulness that the church will be able to arm itself against the inroads of false doctrine.

The message of the church

A right spirit within the church, then, is important for healthy doctrine. But sound teaching—that is, accurate, full and balanced—is also required. This teaching is the revelation of God's mystery, namely Christ, '**in whom are hidden all the treasures of wisdom and knowledge**'.

Paul is about to tell us what he means by that, but already he is asserting that the whole of 'religion' is summed up in Christ. In him all our emotional needs are met; in him both the Christian inclined to mysticism and the one who is only concerned with the practical aspects of the faith, both intellectuals and those with manual skills, find full satisfaction. There is no more enriching experience to be had, no other knowledge to gain, no deeper mystery to fathom, than what we find in him. No wisdom is greater, no knowledge is more necessary, no understanding is more useful, than that which Jesus Christ gives.

Anyone who possesses Jesus Christ — or rather, is possessed by Jesus Christ — has everything. A Christian who turns elsewhere in the hope of increasing his knowledge, his happiness or his experience probably does not know Jesus Christ as he should. He does not yet live in him. He has met him but has not yet got to know him, or else he no longer knows him in the dynamic biblical sense of the word. We do not know a book just because we have scanned the contents page or the preface; in the same way, we do not know a person just because we have met him once or twice. In order really to know him and to be familiar with his ideas and feelings, we have to spend time with him, live with him, walk together with him. Coming back to Christ, Paul therefore goes on, '**So then, just as you received Christ Jesus as Lord, continue to live in him**' (NASB and AV 'walk in him'), together with him. Go on the way you started!

Paul had the privilege of great learning, yet he was declaring near the end of his life, 'I consider everything a loss compared to the surpassing greatness of knowing Christ Jesus my Lord' (Phil. 3:8). 'I want to know Christ', not only through the Scriptures but in my life, through 'the power of his resurrection and the fellowship of sharing in his sufferings' (Phil. 3:10); that is, in actual practice, in a life like his, with a heart in tune with his, victorious with him, suffering with him!

'**Walk in Christ**.' Not just 'with him', but 'in' him. Not wandering here and there in search of new thrills, but '**rooted and built up in him**', '**strengthened**' in what has been given you already — your faith. Not seeking some new idea or teaching, but 'as you were taught'!

The gospel does not need supplementing. Anyway, it has no room for additions. No private revelation, no unusual experience can add anything to it. Our study and our growth must be at a *deep* level, rooted in the gospel, that age-old truth which is always new, that inexhaustible treasury of all wisdom and knowledge. Study and growth must also be on a *practical* level, for true knowledge increases as we simply and joyfully obey what we know.

Contrary to what these Christians in Colosse were inclined to think, nothing could really satisfy their thirst for knowledge or for life—whether a new philosophy, a new mysticism or a new legalism — nothing but Jesus Christ and his eternal gospel. Now as then, he is the only one who can meet the needs of our conscience, reason and heart, the only one who can make our lives full. And that is what salvation is — fulness of life.

11.
Human philosophy or Christ?

Please read Colossians 2:8–10

After an introduction of some length, Paul now comes to the heart of the problem. Up to this point, while expressing his thanks to God, while commending and encouraging the Christians in Colosse, the apostle has only hinted at the error which was threatening the church. Though not yet unmasking it, he has been preparing the remedy; before attacking it, he has been rendering it powerless. When at last he shows it up for what it is, it has already been overcome.

It is by the light of truth that we can discern error. Who would clean a room in the dark? When we have opened the curtains or turned on the light, then the dust shows up and it is easy to get rid of it. On the spiritual level we often have less wisdom, and sometimes we want to get rid of evil or error in someone who is not yet aware of its presence. Condemnation of sin is not enough for a sinner to see it and renounce it. He cannot tell black from white in the dark. Those who walk in darkness cannot recognize sin. So Paul begins by letting in the light; afterwards he condemns the error. First he applies the treatment, then he announces the diagnosis. The logic may be curious, but the psychology is excellent!

Thus, after throwing into relief Christ's glorious majesty and revealing the inexhaustible resources of the Christian, he is about to pinpoint the error, and to attack it by constantly bringing his readers back to the great truth: Christ. 'In him' everything is seen in its true proportions and all victories are won.

Two religions, two ideologies are in confrontation: on one

hand a man-made philosophy, empty, deceptive, and in the last resort barren; on the other a person — Jesus Christ, God incarnate, with whom the Christian has been united by faith, and in whom he shares in the abundance of God's riches.

A human philosophy

The error came in the guise of 'philosophy'. It was no doubt partly because of this name that it held a certain attraction for the Colossians. Paul is not condemning philosophy as such. The word originally denoted 'love of wisdom', and it would be difficult to reject such an idea. Besides, Pythagoras, who is said to have first used the word, taught that no man can be wise, only God[1]. So the idea of philosophy arose amid a feeling that man was inadequate and needed divine revelation. What Paul is condemning is '**hollow and deceptive philosophy which depends on human tradition**', that is, a religious system invented by men and consisting of nothing but subtle and futile speculations. In this system, which the Colossians found so attractive, Christ was dethroned, reduced to the rank of the angels or other spiritual powers, and became merely one of many intermediaries between God and his creation.

Whatever the exact details of this system may have been, it was 'hollow and deceptive'. It was 'hollow' compared with the fulness dwelling in Christ, who is the sum of all wisdom and all knowledge. It was 'deceptive' in that it made people think they were drawing near to God when in fact it was leading them away from him. Such was the nature of this dangerous philosophy, based not on the truths revealed in the Scriptures but on 'human tradition'; it was probably a secret teaching posing as supernatural revelation, and reappeared in various heresies of the early centuries. In the currents of heresy which threatened the church in Colosse and the other

[1] Lightfoot, *op. cit.*, p. 177.

churches of Roman Asia — as is particularly implied in
Paul's letters to Timothy and in John's letters — we detect
the esotericism and the speculations about angelic or cosmic
powers which Gnosticism soon afterwards made popular[2].
When we leave the firm ground of the Scriptures and rely on
personal revelations, anything can happen, all error can be
justified!

Paul goes on to say that this teaching handed down by
men is connected with the '**basic principles**' [*AV* — '**rudi-
ments**'] **of the world**'. What this means is not very clear to
us today. Some have understood it as 'rudimentary instruction' for beginners[3]. This would mean that the Colossians
had mistaken for advanced teaching something which was
only an elementary ABC. The rituals and ceremonies, the
legalism and asceticism they were offered in no way helped
them to progress towards greater spirituality. Far from it!
They were a serious step backwards. How could anything be
added by human effort to the divine completeness which
every Christian possesses through his union with Jesus
Christ? To imagine that anything can be added to it is, in
fact, to belittle the person and work of the Son of God.

But it is more likely that this term belonging to the religious vocabulary of the time had a definite meaning which
the Colossians understood perfectly well. It may well have been
rich in associations with the mythology and astrology of the
Eastern religions which were so popular in this part of Asia
Minor. The 'basic principles of this world' would then be the
forces of the universe, the influence of the stars, and other
supposed powers which superstition has often used to bring

---

[2] The Gnosticism (or more accurately, Gnostic movements) of the second
century onwards had not yet become systematized when Paul was writing,
but the myths, doctrines and rituals characteristic of it had long been
common in the Mediterranean world, especially around Colosse, in Phrygia
where the cult of Cybele began, and in Palestine among the Jewish sect of the
Essenes. (S. Hutin, *'Les Gnostiques'*, Presses Universitaires de France 1970,
pp. 82ff.)

[3] Lightfoot, *op. cit.*, p. 177.

men into bondage[4]. It was not the first time that Paul had
battled with 'principles' of this kind. The Galatians, to whom
he wrote a deeply moving letter, had been slaves to such
principles before coming to know Christ. Having been set
free from these powers by the grace of God, they had been in
danger of succumbing to another, similar yoke: the legalistic
system advocated by a few influential Judaizers. It had been
the same battle, only on another front, against all the powers
that were attempting to take away from Christians their lib-
erty in Christ (Gal. 4:3–10).

Whatever the true meaning may be, writes Paul, any
powers which might exist (whether thrones, powers, rulers or
authorities) are subjected to Christ; better still, Christ has
won the victory over them on the cross. Christ is not a 'principle', a cosmic force; he is over the world, the Creator of all
things. He is not a mere intermediary between God and men,
like the angels; he *is* God, he is 'the fulness of God'. This is
the theme Paul is about to develop.

Christ, the fulness of God

Against this hollow philosophy, this false spirituality, Paul
sets the fulness of God which every Christian united to Jesus
Christ enjoys.

Eternal truth was expressed in many ways throughout the
thousands of years before Christ came. The Old Testament
is a treasure-house of it, with its inspired writings, its symbolic actions and objects, its human lives and yearnings. But
in it the divine light still shone faintly. Only after an eclipse
of several centuries did it shine forth brightly in the apparently never-ending darkness — still veiled, it is true, but
nevertheless present in all its fulness. It appeared in a tangible, physical, human form. The eternal Word 'became flesh
and lived for a while among us. We have seen his glory . . .

---

[4] Hugedé, *op. cit.*, pp. 115ff.

From the fulness of his grace we have all received one blessing after another...No one has ever seen God; but God the
only Son, who is at the Father's side, has made him known'
(John 1:14–18).

'**In Christ all the fulness of the Deity lives in bodily
form**.' He is the long-awaited 'Emmanuel' — God himself
among men (Matt. 1:23). The complete truth is in him: he *is*
the Truth. Christianity rests squarely on this great fact. If it
were not a fact the world would be empty, faith would have
no basis, the gospel would be a hollow sham. But Jesus
Christ is the final, perfect revelation (Heb. 1:2), who has
come to complete all previous revelations of God; he is the
final and only perfect sacrifice, through whom the world is
reconciled once and for all to its Creator (2 Cor. 5:19).

In the light of this divine absolute, all human efforts are
seen in proper perspective; they are but gropings after wisdom, empty dreams, futile ascetic practices, glorification of
fallen men. All intermediaries between man and God are as
nothing when we see the fulness of God revealed in Christ.

Let us take care not to be led astray by new man-made
philosophies nor to put together new religious systems which
only devalue the person and the work of Christ or portray
them as relative. This is the error of those who fall back on
other sources of revelation (such as church traditions and
rules or personal enlightenment), or other means of salvation
(whether the sacraments, self-denial, legalism, asceticism or
good deeds).

'**You have been given fulness in Christ, who is the
head over every power and authority**.' Jesus Christ did
not come into the world just to meet men, to reveal himself
to them, but to live their life, share their existence and, what
is more, to identify himself — to become one — with those
who receive him, so as to enable them to share in his divine
nature (2 Peter 1:4).

In this mysterious union man at last meets his God. If by
faith the Christian is 'in Christ', and if 'in Christ' there lives

all the fulness of God, then the Christian has all the resources of God at his disposal: 'In him you have been made complete' (NASB). Every need, every hope, every longing is more than met.

In the light of this wonderful truth, any addition, any enrichment sought through human traditions or spiritual exercises (even in a spirit of humility) is seen to be an insult to God. The knowledge that we possess such riches 'in Christ' ought to silence for ever all dissatisfaction, grumbling and complaints on the part of Christians.

'Every power and authority', everything that may be placed between God and man, is swept away. Why go on begging favours of subordinates when we receive everything from God himself?

We are now at the core of the epistle: **'In him we have been made complete'** (NASB). If we are aware of this fact, if it is real in our lives, we shall no longer go searching for some novel revelation or hanker after some new experience. God has given us everything: how could men have anything more to offer? As Christians, infinitely rich in Christ, let us no longer dishonour God, his gospel and his church by living like paupers. We should be letting this abundance fill our lives and overflow all around.

12.
A new world

Please read Colossians 2:11–15

The apostle Paul has set out the two basic assertions of Christianity: 'In Christ lives all the fulness of the Deity,' and 'You are in him'. For Jesus Christ is the meeting-point of God and man: this is the heart of the Bible message, the purpose of revelation and redemption. In Jesus Christ, the new man rediscovers God, and with him the fulness of his own being — his freedom, his royal status, his glorious destiny. 'You have been given fulness in Christ.' How wonderful and yet how simple!

Probably the Colossians had not yet taken in all the implications of this tremendous truth. But have the churches of today really grasped them either? Like those first-century Christians, do not we too — though we may not admit it — tend to drift into a 'religion' consisting of traditions, rules, observances, rituals? This reappearance of the natural man can be seen all through the history of the church. The mentality of fallen man keeps surfacing insidiously, irresistibly, within Christianity, producing human religions which are for ever distorting it. Paul realized this dangerous temptation was threatening his friends in Colosse, who still did not fully appreciate the wonderful results of the new life in Christ.

Partial knowledge, or rather, knowledge which is not properly absorbed, is dangerous, for it leaves the heart unsatisfied, and this in turn leads to an unhealthy longing for life in its fulness. If the Christian has not been able to see in the personal fellowship with God which he enjoys *now* in Jesus Christ his most valuable possession and deepest experience, then it will only be outside God's ways that he will go search-

ing for the fulness of life, the 'second blessing' which he feels
he needs. This was the problem of the Colossians, who were
attracted by all kinds of human traditions and philosophies
which they thought were an enrichment to their faith.

So, having shown the superiority of Christ — and thus of
Christianity — over all that might be added, Paul goes
further and states their exclusive nature: when a believer is
united with Christ, he makes a complete break with the old
order and its religious systems.

A complete break

This break, which is as final as death, is particularly well
illustrated by baptism: '**Having been buried with him in
baptism and raised with him through your faith in the
power of God, who raised him from the dead**.' Baptism[1],
which symbolizes burial (confirmation that death has taken
place) and resurrection very well express the transformation
which takes place when we are brought out of the 'dominion
of darkness' into 'the kingdom of the Son [God] loves' (1:13).

Clearly, it is not baptism which produces this fundamental
change; the change is *symbolized* by baptism but *brought about*
in Jesus Christ. It is 'in Christ' that we die and are made
alive. The new life is not born in the baptismal water, but in
the union of the Christian with Christ.

Nor is it faith, we must remember, that brings us from
death to life. Life is not given to us by faith itself but 'by
Christ', to whom faith unites the believer, or 'by the power of
God' demonstrated by Christ's resurrection from the dead.
Life is not given us either by a physical act (baptism) or a
moral one (faith), but by God.

---

[1] By 'baptism' we understand total immersion, because that is undoubtedly
the meaning of the word, because the symbol fits so perfectly the reality it
represents, and because of the preposition which introduces it: 'Buried with
him *in* baptism'.

In order to confirm the deep inward nature of the experience symbolized by baptism, Paul uses the analogy of circumcision: '**In him you were also circumcised, in the putting off of the sinful nature, not with a circumcision done by the hands of men but with the circumcision done by Christ**.' Circumcision was for the Jew a physical sign that he was separated from the world and belonged to the people of God. But in referring to it, the apostle is careful to draw a distinction between this Jewish rite and the reality he wishes to emphasize: he contrasts the physical operation, done by a man, with inner, spiritual circumcision which he compares to 'putting off' or 'shedding'. This shedding of the old way of life ruled by the flesh, that is, by the sinful nature, is not achieved by a sacramental rite or by some ascetic practice, but by Christ, that is, by the power of Christ's life in which the Christian shares.

Total deliverance

The Christian has cut his ties with the past. The powers and authorities — the principles of the universe which formerly held him captive — have no further rights over him; he is quite free from them. And he need not submit to any other authority, tradition or practice that some may try to reimpose on him in the name of a more demanding or more complete 'gospel'. Jesus Christ is not only above all authority, all religious systems; beside him there is no room for them, they stand condemned.

Before proclaiming their total defeat, Paul comes back to the fundamental experience of the Christian. He has just shown that when a believer is united with Christ there occurs a transformation, similar to death followed by resurrection and symbolized by the baptism attested in the gospel. Now he defines a person's condition before and after this transformation: '**When you were dead in your sins and in the**

**uncircumcision of your sinful nature, God made you
alive with Christ**.' The first state is one of death. The word
'death', however, no longer means, as it did before, the *end* of
the old life, but the old life itself considered as a *state* of
spiritual death. It is sin, the expression of a corrupt nature at
enmity with God, that leads to this state of separation from
him which the Bible calls 'death'. The second state is life, the
true life which belongs to eternity; it is a gift of grace, its
source is Christ, it begins when we are forgiven: '**He forgave
us all our sins**.'

The experience which Paul is describing here in terms of
death and life is the same one that he was describing earlier
in terms of enmity and reconciliation: 'Once you were alienated from God and were enemies in your minds because of
your evil behaviour. But now he has reconciled you' (1:21).
In the first case salvation is seen as a practical experience; in
the latter its legal aspect is stressed.

We find this legal aspect again in a further picture used by
Paul to show us the Christian's complete and final break
with the old religious system which had ruled his life until
the new birth — a system which the heretics wanted to bring
back into the church in the form of rules to be kept and
ascetic practices to be observed (2:20–23). This system, this
human philosophy, which enslaves and condemns man, has
been abolished once and for all on the cross: God '**cancelled
out the certificate of debt consisting of decrees against
us and which was hostile to us; and he has taken it out
of the way, having nailed it to the cross**' (NASB). The
meaning of this picture is certainly not as clear for us as it
was for the Colossians.

What is this 'certificate of debt' which God cancelled and
set aside on the cross? Certainly not the law, as it might
appear from some translations. Jesus Christ did not come to
abolish the law, but to fulfil it (Matt. 5:17), to bring it to
perfection by revealing its real and deepest meaning through
his teaching and his life (John 15:11–13; Matt. 22:40; 7:12).

The 'certificate' in question is the document signed by our own hand (as the Greek word indicates), acknowledging our debt to God. By our evil deeds we have, as it were, signed our own condemnation, since these deeds are the indisputable evidence of the evil which dwells in us and separates us from God.

Our debt has been crossed out, not because we paid it off ourselves (an impossibility), but because God's grace has settled it completely and finally. The forgiveness and reconciliation which Christ obtained for us once for all at Calvary become effective when we append another signature, not to a promissory note—which would be foolish—but to an acknowledgement of debt, admitting our own insolvency.

The cross has put an end to our condemnation; more than this, it puts an end to all bondage: '**Having disarmed the powers and authorities, he made a public spectacle of them, triumphing over them by the cross**.' This picture of a conqueror's triumphal procession, with the defeated enemies being paraded at the rear, is full of meaning. The cross is Christ's victory over all man-made religious systems which offer a way to God while actually leading men astray.

The Christian has entered a new world through spiritual resurrection; his baptism bears witness to this. 'In Christ' he is henceforth freed from the tyranny and burden of sin; freed too from all religious systems which have claimed they could save him from it[2].

The old world is dead, irrevocably dead. Christ is the way that leads to God: he is the only meeting-point, the only mediator between God and man. Any addition diminishes him; any 'enriched' gospel is a 'different' gospel. Nothing surpasses Christ, 'in whom we have been made complete'.

---

[2] False teachers tried to do this by imposing on the Colossians rules about 'good deeds' and ascetic practices.

13.
Natural religion

Please read Colossians 2:16–23

The apostle Paul continues to work out the implications of Christ's total sufficiency, which was more than enough to overcome the syncretism to which the Colossians were attracted. The desire for progress in the spiritual life — a healthy motive in itself — can lead the Christian along a dangerous path. Instead of seeking this progress by studying the revealed truths more deeply and practising them joyfully, he may be tempted to explore avenues foreign to the gospel, or to get at the truth by observing practices more sophisticated than scriptural revelation warrants.

In so doing, he would drift imperceptibly from the worship of God to the worship of man, he would discard the freedom won by Jesus Christ over all the forces which held him captive, and subject himself to another oppressive yoke (Gal. 4:9, 10; 5:1; 3:3). Paul sees this danger, which has three closely linked aspects: legalism, mysticism and asceticism. It is difficult to draw the line between them, but we shall deal with them separately so as to make it easier to analyse the different elements of an ever-present temptation.

Legalism

In every generation legalism has played havoc in the churches, often in the best ones. This disease especially attacks evangelical Christianity, the churches and Christians who are most devoted to the Bible and have high ideals and great zeal for God.

The complaint is all the more dangerous because it shows up differently in different people. Generally speaking, one person has a legalistic attitude about a few particular issues, while other people have scruples about different points. These legalistic codes, which vary with individuals, churches, times and places, come into conflict, stirring up criticism and divisions. Although they are mainly concerned with matters of secondary importance, they almost always cause serious rifts.

In Colosse, as indeed in Rome (Rom. 14:1–6), the dispute was not on a point of doctrine but about religious practices relating to food and festivals: '**Do not let anyone judge you by what you eat or drink, or with regard to a religious festival, a new moon celebration or a Sabbath day. These are a shadow of the things that were to come; the reality, however, is found in Christ**.'

Judaism, with its regulations concerning food and ritual, laid a considerable burden on the first Christian churches, causing sharp conflicts within them (as in the churches in Rome and Galatia) or between them (the churches of Antioch and Jerusalem). These regulations, whether laid down by God or added by men, were only the shadow of things to come; they pointed to, or prepared the way for, the revelation of the *reality* to be found in Christ and perhaps especially in the 'body of Christ'. This is confirmed in the letter to the Hebrews: 'This is an illustration for the present time, indicating that the gifts and sacrifices being offered were not able to clear the conscience of the worshipper. They are only a matter of food and drink and various ceremonial washings — external [human] regulations applying only until the time of the new order [which Jesus Christ came to establish]. When Christ came . . .', he accomplished once and for all what the Jewish religion prefigured (Heb. 9:9–11).

It seems, however, that in Colosse the difficulties were caused more by pagan practices than by Jewish regulations. In fact, what Paul says could apply just as well to either.

Paganism had its annual festivals and its new moons, associated with fasting. These religious practices, just as much as those of the Jews, were to some extent a shadow[1] of the reality which came with Jesus Christ. As Paul recognized when addressing the Athenians (Acts 17:27), they meant that people were waiting for—groping for—an unknown truth beyond the grasp of the human mind. Whether pagan or Jew, whether living in the first or twentieth century, everyone is more or less consciously (though sometimes he will not admit it) searching for the God in whose image he was made.

But in any case, whether we are talking of Mosaic rites — divinely inspired or deformed by tradition — or else of pagan practices resulting from man's ignorance (Rom. 1:20–23), the shadow, the copy, has given way to reality. Salvation, to which these types were pointing, the goal for which man was groping, is fully and finally realized in Jesus Christ. So to follow shadows, when reality is present in Christ, would be a retrograde step. What would we say if a bride-to-be who has waited a long time for the return of the man she loves, looks away from him, when at last he comes back, to gaze at his portrait on her bedside table? Is this not the attitude of the legalist who, so taken up with the shadows of the law, has forgotten the one who was there to satisfy all his longings?

It is absolutely necessary to organize our lives, to have rules of conduct and strict discipline, if we are to serve efficiently (1 Cor. 9:24–27); faithfulness in little things is a sign of faithfulness in everything. But if we are not careful, all this soon degenerates into a legalism which warps the Christian life, puts burdens on others and produces hypocrisy. 'It is for freedom that Christ has set us free. Stand firm, then, and do not let yourselves be burdened again by a yoke of slavery' (Gal. 5:1). Here Paul is, of course, speaking of the freedom

---

[1] This image, used in the letter to the Hebrews (8:5; 9:23; 10:1), was very common in pagan antiquity (N. Hugedé, *op. cit.*, p. 145).

which Christ gives — the power to do what is right and good, the only true freedom there can be.

A Christian's only law, insists the apostle, is Christ (1 Cor. 9:21): Christ revealed in the Word given and interpreted by the Holy Spirit.

Mysticism

Throughout his letter Paul is fighting the temptation among the Colossians to add to the gospel and thus to corrupt it. This temptation is seen not only in legalism, but also in a kind of mysticism going with it: '**Do not let anyone who delights in false humility and the worship of angels disqualify you for the prize. Such a person goes into great detail about what he has seen [taking his stand on visions he has seen, NASB] and his unspiritual mind puffs him up with idle notions. He has lost connection with the Head**' (2:18).

Someone, whose name is not mentioned, seemed to be trying to lead the church towards a kind of asceticism: we shall deal with this later. The worship he proposes has an appearance of great humility; its attraction lies in a spirit of self-denial and mortification, and it is quite in keeping with the attitude of the natural man before the greatness and holiness of God. In all ages men have been afraid to meet God and have tried to gain his favour through good deeds, personal sacrifices, or mediators intervening on their behalf. To claim that one is able to pray to God directly or have fellowship with him without the help of a go-between is often considered presumptuous and arrogant; and some think that to go straight to Jesus Christ himself is to show lack of respect and humility.

In fact, the exact opposite is true. To replace the simplicity of the gospel by a man-made religious system, even with the best of intentions, to substitute one's personal feelings and reasonings for the word of Christ, is not humility but pride. When we disregard God's revelation of himself in the Bible and attach importance to visions or private revelations — whether our own or other people's, whether real or imaginary—we are leaving the firm ground of a truth which has been tested, confirmed, substantiated over thousands of years, and moving into the dangerous quicksands of human wisdom, imagination or imposture.

Outside the Word of God is the realm of private religion, thrills, error and sectarianism. To a certain extent it is also outside the church, for the church is responsible for seeing that we have a right understanding of God's Word and a complete grasp of its riches (Eph. 3:18; 4:11–14). This latter idea may not be far from Paul's mind when he writes, 'The reality, however, is found in Christ', literally, 'but the body is of Christ' (2:17). There is probably more here than the contrast between reality — 'the body' — and shadow; there may well be a reference to the 'body of Christ' as a protection against all mysticism. Spiritual growth does not come from religious practices but from the Head, Jesus Christ, in union with his body, the church (2:19).

Asceticism

The religious system or 'philosophy' which threatened the Colossians had a doctrinal aspect: in particular, the heretics attributed great importance to invisible beings or powers (angels, basic principles of the world). But it matters little whether these were real or imaginary, useful or hostile, borrowed from Judaism or from paganism: it was and always will be impossible to worship or fear them while at the same time worshipping Jesus Christ, who is the ultimate reality and truth, whose power is supreme.

This system also had its practical side. The asceticism it proposed as a means to attain a higher life was the logical outcome of the combination of legalism and mysticism. It derived its method from legalism and its inspiration from mysticism, both of them being in direct contradiction with the truths of the gospel.

'**Do not handle! Do not taste! Do not touch!**' How numerous are these religious prohibitions, how popular are these superstitions which enslave countless people — sometimes even Christians! In the present context these refer to perishable things, which in themselves have no importance and nothing to do with the kingdom of God (Rom. 14:17). What *is* important, however, is the way they are used — or rather, not used. These taboos are not neutral, since they are presented as conditions for holiness: '**Such regulations indeed have an appearance of wisdom, with their self-imposed worship, their false humility and their harsh treatment of the body, but they lack any value in restraining sensual indulgence.**' The high state of spirituality of those who observe such rules of piety is only apparent. What is really behind this spiritual front is not the worship of Jesus Christ but the worship of man, invented by man and flattering his pride and his ego or gratifying his passions.

Religion which finds its expression in all kinds of self-imposed sacrifices or mortification has less in common with Christianity than with the dualistic religions which asserted the superiority of the spirit and despised the body. Such a religion, imbued with human and pagan ideas, has nothing to do with the gospel of the grace of God[2].

[2] The church did not escape this danger foreseen by Paul. 'Throughout the second century A.D., with few exceptions, the dynamic power of *agape* was to some extent paralysed by the formality and constraint of Jewish pietism and Hellenic asceticism . . . What originally was often just an incidental result of a deep inward conversion now became the prevailing element, and was sometimes cut off from the spirit which alone gave it meaning. We have seen that as early as New Testament times various ascetic groups had combined faith with their old ideal of abstinence. Later this principle, in all its forms, became universally accepted as the inspiration and source of all virtue.' (R. Minnerath, *Les chrétiens dans le monde, Ier et IIe siècles*, pp. 265ff). 'Self-control'

No human achievement, no personal sacrifice has any merit before God. To credit even the finest, noblest, most selfless human action with any value is to sin against the majesty and love of God. For it means to envisage putting pressure on God's sovereignty, a quite intolerable idea; it means despising the unique, perfect, infinite and final sacrifice made by Jesus Christ on the cross; it means setting up man's religion in the place of God's revelation.

No doubt personal discipline is essential in any kind of dedication, and loving service will inevitably involve sacrifice and hardship. But the Christian must be careful not to confuse the fruit of the Spirit with the works of the flesh which, apart from their futility in God's eyes, may only serve to satisfy the natural man.

The gospel is fulness of life, free and without limit. For the gospel *is* Jesus Christ. Christ is the end of *legalism* for he is the end of the law (Rom. 10:4), in the sense that, by leading us to Jesus Christ, the law has achieved its purpose and also that those who are 'in Christ' are no longer condemned by it (Rom. 8:1). Christ is the remedy for *mysticism*. Those who have found everything in Christ no longer need to seek other knowledge or experiences elsewhere: Christ and his Word are completely sufficient. Christ is the negation of *asceticism*. His sacrifice is fully sufficient for our salvation, and trying to add any sacrifice of our own would be to challenge the power of the cross (Heb. 10:14). Let us then live fully and positively, in the freedom and joy given by God, that is, in obedience to his Word and in the 'friendship' of Jesus Christ (John 15:15).

'Jesus Christ and him crucified': Paul's whole message and his whole life are centred on the person and work of Jesus Christ. Christ is both God's answer to man's need and the end of all man-made religious systems. This is the meaning of the first part of the Epistle to the Colossians which we have just examined.

(*encrateia*) became abstinence and continence; the gospel of grace was replaced by a negative morality.

Jesus Christ is also the inspiration for all our Christian living. This is the theme of the second part which begins in chapter 3 of the epistle.

14.
A hidden life

Please read Colossians 3:1–4

The first two chapters of the letter are concerned with doctrinal matters centred on the person and work of Jesus Christ. Paul's method of dealing with them comes out of his great desire to fight the error threatening the church in Colosse, and to defend the truth. This concern, noticeable from the start, has become still clearer towards the end of the second chapter with its distinctly polemical tone.

Paul's train of thought is masterly and deserves closer attention. He does not plunge straight into the problems which were probably the reason for this letter. They are in his mind, but he is not in a hurry to raise them. His whole argument is centred on the gospel and on grace: this is the light which scatters darkness, the life which conquers death (2 Cor. 5:4), the love which banishes fear (1 John 4:18), the new life which replaces the old, the fulness of the Spirit which holds our carnal nature in check. The gospel is not a moral code, but a living power; Christianity is not a religion — it is Jesus Christ. Jesus Christ, the *Truth*, is the one who removes *error* as his light shines in men's hearts: this is what the first part of the epistle has shown us. Also, Jesus Christ is the *Life* which, as it flows into the hearts of men, triumphs over *evil*: this is what we shall find as we study the second part of the epistle dealing more with practical matters.

The first four verses of chapter 3 are both a fitting conclusion to what has gone before, and an excellent introduction to what is to come.

The source of the Christian life

'Since, then, you have been raised with Christ, set your hearts on things above.' We are often tempted to think of the Christian life in terms of its negative side — that of dying to the old self, which brings to mind separation, renunciation, sacrifice. However, that is not how Paul presents it at first. Later, of course, he brings us inevitably, with the balance that always characterizes his teaching, to the painful realities of permanent death to self. But these realities — negative, it is true — have to be seen in the positive light of Christ's resurrection and our own new life in him.

Before condemning certain sins in the lives of the Colossians — and consequently in our lives, too — Paul lifts his brothers' hearts and minds towards the heavenly realities, towards Christ, who is the source of true life. It is not by fighting sin, the world and the flesh on their own ground that the Colossians will overcome them, not by using the human means which Paul has been condemning, but by rising above them.

'You have been raised with Christ', you have been made to share in the very life of Christ, you are now citizens of a different world. If this is true, if this is your experience, then your whole life is changed. You can no longer see things as the world sees them, you can no longer fight evil as the world fights it.

Before, your life drew on itself for strength, found inspiration in its own ideas and was only motivated by its own interests; but since Christ has met you on your way, now that he has taken hold of you, it draws on him for strength, inspiration and meaning. Your life, essentially earthbound, has found a new, vertical dimension: God has given it an opening above, through which his own life breaks through and your desires can at last rise to find their highest goal and perfect fulfilment.

The sphere of the Christian life

How does this affect our everyday lives? 'Where your
treasure is, there your heart will be also' (Matt. 6:21). Once
our treasure, our interests, our purpose in life were earthly,
our hearts were set on the things of this world, whether good
or bad. Now that he has saved us, Christ has become the
goal of our lives, and our eyes have followed him to where he
sits at God's right hand. Our interest, our purpose and our
heart are now where Christ is. **'Set your hearts on things
above, where Christ is seated at the right hand of God.'**

It is not natural for the human heart to be concerned with
heavenly things, to act always with a spiritual purpose, to
think of everything in terms of the eternal and the invisible,
and this can become very hard for someone who wants to be
religious but has never met Jesus Christ personally.

It is different for those who have found everything in
Christ! What was against our nature now becomes perfectly
natural. In the new birth we were born into a new life; in
baptism we showed that we had died to the old life and
wanted to live for Christ. So we seek him, we come to him
where he is, we love what he loves; his thoughts are our
thoughts, his interests are our interests, his concerns are our
concerns — the things which are above.

This pursuit of spiritual matters, this concern with God's
interests, testify to the reality of conversion. If anyone claims
to be a Christian but has the same preoccupations as
everyone else, if his life is earthbound, if he is not gripped by
a high ideal and shows no inclination for eternal realities and
values, then he is deluding himself. Does not an exile yearn
for his homeland? If we are 'born from above' (John 3:3), we
cannot help longing for the things above.

But does that mean that we despise the earth, that we
regard with indifference and scorn the world in which we are
clearly placed? Is *heaven* a place to which to escape? One

might almost think so, to judge by some Christians whose feet seem no longer to be touching the ground, so to speak, who are so intent on heavenly things that they lose touch with the here and now. Is the hope of heaven a kind of opium, a drug making it possible to have a 'trip' into another world and so get relief from the troubles of this one?

This is not in Paul's mind at all. The Christian life is not a double one in which there is a constant tug of war between contradictory interests and desires — heavenly on one hand, earthly on the other. It cannot be emphasized too often: there is no dualistic conflict in the Christian life.

The Christian life is *life* itself, perfectly integrated. It does not mean heaven *against* earth, but heaven *on* earth: the things above in the things of earth, the concerns of heaven in the pursuits of men, God in the midst of our human life and problems. To live the Christian life is to live fully each moment of our existence on earth in terms of the realities and values of heaven; it is to live to the full one's personal, family and working life in the awareness that they continue and find their fulfilment beyond the earthly, the visible, the tangible, in the invisible and the eternal. *Spiritual* life is not life on the level of the *spirit* (as opposed to the body), but total life (human and practical), inspired, directed and controlled by the *Holy Spirit*. The apostle will develop this idea a little further on. This new dimension gives to every moment of life its right proportions and its true value.

The mystery of the Christian life

Seen in this light, it is easier to understand Paul's reflection: **'You died, and your life is now hidden with Christ in God**.' For there is an element of mystery about this life. It cannot be understood by those who do not know God and do not have this vertical dimension. The Christian life, which finds its motivation in God, in Christ, in things 'above', out-

side its own experience, and which seeks eternal and divine
goals far beyond its own field of vision, makes no sense to the
man of the world.

So if a Christian is mourning he weeps, but without losing
hope. If he is successful he does not see in this the result of
his own ability or skill, but humbly attributes his success to
God. In failure he does not despair; in wealth he does not fall
victim to pride or extravagance; in poverty he gives; if
wronged, he does not think of revenge. Such a life is folly to
the world, which cannot see its hidden source and goal or its
guiding principles, and does not realize its strength.

'You *died*': you have passed beyond this world, beyond its
comprehension; it cannot follow you to the other side of
death. 'Flesh gives birth to flesh, but the Spirit gives birth to
spirit . . . The wind blows wherever it pleases. You hear its
sound, but you cannot tell where it comes from or where it is
going. So it is with everyone born of the Spirit' (John 3:6–8).
This is the mystery of the life in Christ, that hidden life
renewed at the eternal springs of communion with Christ; it
is like an unexpected oasis in the middle of a parched desert,
quite inexplicable if one only looks at the surface, but fed by
an invisible watercourse in the midst of a barren waste.

Happy is the man who sets his heart on things above,
whose 'delight is in the law of the Lord and on his law he
meditates day and night. He is like a tree planted by streams
of water, . . . whose leaf does not wither' (Psalm 1:2–3).

The revelation of the Christian life

But this enigmatic, indefinable life, which baffles the world's
understanding and often our own, will one day reveal its
mystery, its hidden meaning. Christ has taken it with him,
beyond death, into another world; it is thus beyond all
analysis. But Christ will return and reveal this life that is
hidden in him. '**When Christ, who is your life, appears,**

then you also will appear with him in glory.'

Christ is *life*; not merely the source and the purpose of life, but life itself. So when he appears the world will discover the real life, while all too often the image we reflect of it in our own existence is blurred, distorted, faded, weak and stained with sin. When he appears, all things will be made new: creation will rediscover its purpose, its meaning; life will display its infinity and its glory.

Our destiny is linked to Christ's for ever! Having died with him and been raised to life with him, we shall suffer with him, but also one day we shall appear with him and his glory will be our glory. His coming will show up all the emptiness of 'earthly things' and finally justify faithfulness to the 'things above'. So we are brought back to the centre of everything — Jesus Christ, through whom and for whom all things exist, in whom all things have their being.

Instead, then, of trying to live the Christian life by human means, under the burden of intolerable legalism or useless asceticism, instead of paying attention to all these 'earthly things' which raise us no higher than the earth, let us fix our eyes on things above, where Christ is seated at the right hand of God. And all these things above, all heaven itself, are summed up in a single word, a single person — Christ.

Let us look to him, and everything will be seen again in true perspective. Then, armed with his victorious power, we shall be able to stand up to the attacks of sin, the flesh and the world, and face the problems and struggles of life which Paul deals with next.

15.
Life against death

Please read Colossians 3:5–11

If the apostle Paul has lifted our thoughts above the visible into the very presence of God, where our life is hidden with Christ, it is to bring us more firmly down to earth, to our human existence in the world, where a battle is always going on.

He has just made us aware of the tension which exists between the imperfections of the Christian life as lived on earth and the perfection of the *same* life which will be revealed when Christ appears in his glory. But there is more than just a tension between the present and the future; there is an all-out, agonizing conflict between the present and the past, between righteousness and sin, between the new life springing from the union of the Christian with Christ and the old life which has its source in the corrupt human heart.

The life which is 'hidden with Christ in God' is not lived in lofty and peaceful spiritual realms, far from the bustle of the world, sheltered from the temptation of sin, from suffering and death, but on the battlefield of this earth, where our Lord himself had to fight in order to overcome. 'The life I live *in the body*, I live by faith in the Son of God, who loved me and gave himself for me' (Gal. 2:20). So, having climbed to the bright mountain top, from where we had a distant view of the glory to come, we now go down again into the valley where the merciless fight is going on, but where our life, hidden with Christ in God, also has to be lived.

'You died' (3:3): this was not, as might be supposed, the signal that the war was over, but the call to arms: '**Put to death, therefore ...!**'

The enemy

The enemy is sin. But sin has many forms, and Paul is not content with declaring war on sin in general. He knows what human nature is like, and knows perfectly well that we — and that includes Christians, alas! — could easily take advantage of the vagueness of the word to give it the meaning which suits us, that is, the one which puts us most at ease.

He exposes some of the commonest sins of his day — and apparently of any age — calling them by name. He portrays them metaphorically as the different 'parts' of the old man, of the old nature: 'Put to death therefore the parts of your body which are on the earth' (literal translation from the Greek). He thus defines the battleground clearly: sin is not outside us, but in us. It is easy to condemn the world as the source of sin and to attack it in all its outward manifestations, but it is first and foremost an *inner* enemy.

Moreover — and Paul stresses this very strongly by the image of the body and its constituent parts — the enemy is not only within us, but is intimately bound up with every fibre of our being. The enemy is so much an integral part of us that we cannot strike him without striking ourselves, nor condemn him without condemning ourselves, nor put him to death without dying ourselves. We can see at once how subtle, difficult and fierce this war is, for the fight against sin is a fight against ourselves.

In the light of this awesome truth, we can now see why the moral rules and ascetic practices to which Paul referred previously are totally inadequate. Either they make the sincere and conscientious person despair, for he has in the end to admit defeat; or else they serve to glorify man, but with the final result that, though he has won a few battles, he has lost the war. 'If it is the old man which has mutilated the old man . . ., several enemies have merely been sacrificed to a single enemy. To one sin, a great sin, a powerful sin, the first

of all sins — self-will — have been added all the rest'[1]. But
we shall return to the particular nature of this conflict after
identifying the enemy: the various sins, which can be divided
into two groups.

The first includes sins concerning the *individual himself*,
especially in relation to his body: **'Put to death therefore ... sexual immorality, impurity, lust, evil desires
and greed, which is idolatry.'** In this list the apostle moves
from the crudest and most obvious sin (immorality) to the
subtlest (greed). There ought to be no room for such things in
the church. Paul makes it clear that this kind of behaviour
should be a thing of the past for the Christians in Colosse:
**'You used to walk in these ways, in the life you once
lived.'**

The first four sins need no comment, they are so blatantly
contradictory to the holiness of God. But the last one, greed,
deserves consideration because of its subtlety. Note the
dreadful term with which it is coupled. This 'idolatry' is
sometimes difficult to unmask, being hidden behind deceptive appearances such as caution, economy or prudence. It is
said that Francis of Sales, who heard the confession of many
penitents, never came across anyone who accused himself of
greed! Yet this sin arouses 'the wrath of God' no less than
the others. 'These enemies are all the more dangerous as
they were once our constant friends!'[2]

The second group of sins is more concerned with the *relationship between Christians:* **'Now you must rid yourselves of
all such things as these: anger, rage, malice, slander and
filthy language from your lips.'** These sins, which we consider less serious according to our human scale of values, are
no more excusable than the previous ones, and yet they often
keep a foothold in our churches where they do incalculable
damage.

[1] A. Vinet: *Etudes et Méditations Evangéliques I*, p. 348.

[2] A. Vinet, *op. cit.*, p. 341.

In addition to these culpable attitudes — for sins of this kind generally harden into permanent frames of mind — there is lying: '**Do not lie to each other**.' It is not only the spoken lie that is meant here, but more particularly deceptive behaviour. It is common in the church, unfortunately, to try to appear what one is not, to give the impression of being more spiritual than one really is, to pretend not to have temptations, doubts, fears, failures and bad thoughts — in short, to deny that the old, sinful nature is still there despite one's conversion. We are ashamed to admit that! And yet to admit it could bring liberation to some Christians who feel discouraged at our apparent holiness and may themselves be tempted to be untruthful so as not to look as if they are lagging behind!

The path to victory

How can man destroy enemies which are within him, which are part of himself? How could a country win a war if its whole army, indeed its whole population, were in the pay of the enemy? To destroy sin amounts to destroying the sinner!

We try to make a distinction between sin and the sinner, but although this is easy enough in theory, it is not so in practice. The radical method, at which we tremble, the divine method, is the only logical one in the end: 'You died!' Everything in us was incurably defiled, every fibre of our being was permanently corrupt: death was the only answer. And it is true, we are *dead in Christ*; when Christ died, we died with him. So we must confirm this death every day and let it be a practical reality each moment of the inevitable battle.

But how can a dead man come alive and win the victory? In fact, anyone who has died with Christ has also been *raised to life with Christ*, by the power of his life (2:12). This new force coming into action will keep in check the conquered power of sin; the law of the Spirit of life will set us free from sin's law of gravity. This new life will drive out the old, like a flow of fresh, living water irresistibly sweeping away the foul, stagnant waters which only harboured death.

Just as sin had permeated all our being and taken control of every part of us, of all our faculties, so our new Master, Jesus Christ, will take possession of them in his turn (Rom. 6:19). And life will drive out death: 'What is mortal [will] be swallowed up by life' (2 Cor. 5:4). The source of this life is indeed 'hidden with Christ in God', but the life itself springs up and flows within us to cleanse and transform us. This life cannot stay hidden. The gospel is not a theory; being a Christian is not just a matter of subscribing to a certain creed. The gospel is a power, a life which, having conquered death, pursues it into all its hiding places and washes away all its stains.

To be a Christian is to live out this terrible struggle between life and death, it is to experience this sure and steady victory of life over death. As the old self dies, '**the new self is being renewed**'. Or rather, the natural self retreats under the continual pressure of the irresistible life that is in Christ. That life which burst open the sealed tomb on Easter Day is available to us here and now. It is this life which is at work in man — defiled, deformed and ruined by sin — remaking and re-creating him '**in the image of [his] Creator**', so as to bring him to the highest knowledge of all, to a bond of fellowship with God who *is* life, and life eternal.

So the gospel presented in the Scriptures is not a law which crushes man by asking the impossible of him, but a living power which breaks through into the depths of his being to purify, regenerate and restore him so that he can follow his true calling as a man, to the glory of his Creator.

And this life goes still further: it carries us towards a new society which all mankind is waiting for, promised by many political systems and many religions, only to vanish in bloodshed; a society of justice and peace where there is no longer '**Greek or Jew, circumcised or uncircumcised, barbarian, Scythian, slave or free**', that is, where there are no more racial, religious, cultural or social barriers because Christ is all things for all people.

The whole creation yearns for such a humanity, such a society. But these can only come about if the world gives up its old untrustworthy friends and breaks up its idols. We are living in an idolatrous world where everyone toils and fights to hold on to his gods of iron, wood, stone, gold or flesh; we live in an impure, greedy world; our hearts — and sometimes our mouths — are full of malice. We are fettered by our passions and dragged towards death, powerless. But God has not given us up. He has remembered us; he has come; he has passed through death in order to give us life, an irresistible torrent of life which death will soon be swallowed up.

16.
From love to peace

Please read Colossians 3:12–15

In the previous section Paul reminded us of a painful but necessary duty of putting to death all forms of sin, of renunciation and self-emptying. He set before us a grim, daunting task, an endless struggle! But he also showed us the way this can be done, he told us the secret of success: the new life which God puts within us and which, by its constant renewal, will conquer death, take back stolen territory and regain the authority that rightly belonged to it. Out of the death of the old self rises the new personality.

The act of self-emptying was just the *negative* side of the work of sanctification which God carries out in the Christian's life, and for which he asks our full co-operation. Now we are shown the other side, the *positive* side, of this work. After the taking off comes the putting on, the reclothing; after the sins come the virtues. Into the heart of man Satan put sin, the root of all individual sins; by the new birth God implants love, the root and principle of a new life. Sin has divided men and poisoned all human relations; love will build a society without class and restore all human relationships in the peace of Christ.

Love, the divine principle which Jesus Christ, by his incarnation and death, has put back into the heart of the world and of man, is the only power able to win the victory over sin and all its bondage. The secret of taking off the old self lies in putting on the new self. 'Renewal comes through love; to be born again is to love, in the full meaning of that word in the gospel. If then the new man puts to death whatever belongs to his earthly nature . . ., it is because he loves and only because he loves. This is the way above all others to win this war of extermination... it is the simplest, surest way, the only way that is sure, true and deep. No other penetrates to the depths; no other sees the depths. Only love exterminates... love is insatiable, love is intolerant, love is destructive, love is never satisfied till it has exterminated sin.'[1]

But before showing in detail what it means to 'put on love', Paul points out the decisive motive that should inspire us to take a willing, active part in the work of God: '**Therefore, as God's chosen people, holy and dearly loved...**' Every privilege involves a responsibility, and every blessing a duty. Therefore much is expected of those whom God has chosen and set apart to be the objects of his love; from those who have received everything, much will be required. Besides, much *can* be expected of them; for those who have received all, in such a way, and who know it, are ready to give everything.

The Christian's new clothes

Since from now on you are new people, show your new life, express it openly. As you strip off the miserable rags of sin, put on the glorious garments of love. And Paul mentions five of the most typical Christian virtues and explains how they should show themselves in human relationships: '**Clothe yourselves with compassion, kindness, humility, gentleness and patience.**' They all originate in love, which binds them together into a perfect whole; they all have peace as their aim.

First he exhorts the Christian to 'clothe himself with *compassion*'. Compassion for others is a typically Christian virtue. The Christian is conscious more than anyone else of the plight of the world, in which, behind men's physical and

[1] A. Vinet, *op. cit.*, pp. 359ff.

moral troubles, he sees their spiritual ruin. The Christian's genuine joy always goes together with deep sorrow, for he cannot be indifferent to the world's sufferings. While continually rejoicing at the riches which were his in Christ, Paul had 'great sorrow and unceasing anguish' in his heart at the thought of his lost brothers, those of his own race (Rom. 9:2).

Next we are called to *kindness*, which leads us to seek the well-being of others. Since God has given us his love so richly, our happiness will be to share this love with others. Just as God has shown concern for us, his children, so we shall show concern for others, and the love we have received will flow on to them. The kindness spoken of here is a disposition of the mind and heart, a loving care for others; it forgets any faults in them, it covers over their wrongdoing and seeks their well-being.

Thirdly, there is *humility*. Indeed, there can be no real kindness without humility. Before we can show real concern for others we must forget about ourselves, about our rights, or the consideration we might expect to be given. One must have a modest opinion of oneself in order not to be afraid of being humbled. Did not Jesus lose his reputation and his honour in the world's eyes by being the friend of tax-collectors, sinners and people of low morals, by showing them his concern and his kindness?

Gentleness again is a 'loving' virtue, very close to compassion and kindness. Gentleness spares others anything which might distress or hurt them. It is the opposite of sternness and harshness. But, since it springs from real love, it is a strong virtue which has nothing to do with sentimentality.

Finally, there is *patience*, which enables the Christian not to flare up at the slightest provocation, not to get downhearted at the least disappointment. The Christian must be able to endure without feelings of revenge, to wait and hope against all odds. Patience enables him to stand firm and remain kind and gentle despite the rebuffs, ingratitude and unpleasantness of other people.

These five virtues will be expressed and will complement one another in the context of a community where there is tolerance and forgiveness; this is essential to the harmony of the body of Christ: **'Bear with each other and forgive whatever grievances you may have against one another. Forgive as the Lord forgave you.'**

To *bear with* each other is to accept one's brothers and sisters just as they are, with all their weaknesses and shortcomings. It is not always easy! We wish — quite rightly — they were so much better than they are: more loving, more understanding, more gentle, more patient, more hospitable, more generous, more reliable, more punctual, more open . . . It is not easy to put up with the irritations, the criticisms, the harsh or bitter words, the unfairness which some of our brothers can inflict on us. They are not perfect; neither is the church. But it cannot live without this acceptance, this mutual tolerance, which is the fruit of compassion, kindness, humility, gentleness and patience.

Nor can the church live without *forgiveness*: '*Forgive* whatever grievances you may have against *one another*' so as to preserve unity, or to restore it when it has been broken. Christian relationships cannot exist without this true forgiveness from the heart. We ourselves should still be under God's anger if he had not truly forgiven us at the cross. All the many and great grievances he had against us he has nailed to the cross, torn up and forgotten for ever.

But God does more than wipe our record clean; when we have been forgiven he pours out on us all the riches of his grace. Vinet sees this very clearly: 'In order really to forgive, one must do more than forgive: evil must be overcome by good and, following God's own example, where there is much sin there must be much more grace.'[2] Christ's forgiveness is the motive and pattern of the forgiveness we owe our brothers: 'Just as the Lord forgave you, so also should you' (NASB).

[2] A. Vinet: *Premières Méditations Evangéliques*, p. 202.

Love

'And over all these virtues put on love, which binds them all together in perfect unity.' There is no more hackneyed word than 'love'. It is the only value for which the world might still have some respect, but is all too often associated with what is most base, superficial, short-lived and selfish on earth. It is not in such caricatures of love, but in God who *is* love — the source and pattern of love — that we discover its real meaning. The Bible gives us far more than a definition of love — which would be impossible — it gives us an actual demonstration of this divine virtue which we are called to show in our relations with others. John goes to the heart of the matter: 'This is how we know what love is: Jesus Christ laid down his life for us. And we ought to lay down our lives for our brothers' (1 John 3:16).

Love, then, is not a feeling but an *act*. It is not a response to someone else's love, it is given without expecting anything in return: 'This is love: not that we loved God, but that he loved us' (1 John 4:10). In other words, contrary to what we often think, love does not grow spontaneously from a feeling of affinity or out of mere personal attraction; it is *willed*: it overcomes dislike, it goes out to the ungrateful. While human love is often ruled by taste, whim, self-interest and chance, it is the will that is uppermost in divine love, that will which is God's grace. The reason for love is only found in God. When we were still powerless, sinful, even enemies, God showed his love for us by giving his own Son to reconcile us to himself and stir up love in us (Rom. 5:6–10). It is just because love between brothers and sisters, or husbands and wives, is not of that kind, that it often fails miserably: we expect to get something instead of giving ourselves. Love is measured by the cross!

It also begins at the cross when, united to Jesus Christ by faith, we are crucified to ourselves and the world, when our self-centredness has been overcome and we have renounced our way of thinking, which till now has been moulded by the world. The knowledge of love can come to us not only as we *contemplate* God and the cross, but as we *experience* the cross which sets us free from our superficial way of life.

This is the love which is the power behind compassion, kindness, humility, gentleness and patience — which together make tolerance and forgiveness possible in the church. It is the bond between all these virtues, for it is the root they spring from. We may very much want to possess one or other of these qualities, but when we have love we have all of them at once. They are just different expressions of love. Perfection is not in this or that virtue but in all of them together. And it is love which completes and perfects each of them, binding them together in perfect harmony. That is why Paul writes elsewhere that if he has no love he *has* nothing and *is* nothing (1 Cor. 13:1–3).

Peace

In the church the outcome of these expressions of love will be peace: '**Let the peace of Christ rule in your hearts, since as members of one body you were called to peace**' — peace in the heart and peace in the church.

Can the heart be at peace when bitterness, accusations, grievances and disagreements exist in the church? These things which we tolerate, which we so often just get used to, kill the joy of prayer, of Bible study and fellowship; they make spiritual life dry up, they halt its progress, they undermine its witness. Sacrificial, self-giving love is the one condition for peace of heart and conscience. Peace is to the soul what health is to the body: a sign of balance and order, and also the condition for full growth and development. It only comes fully when man is himself at peace with God through the reconciliation accomplished in Christ.

And only when each individual member enjoys this health

will peace reign in the body, the church. 'If one part suffers, every part suffers with it.' Let us not delude ourselves: the church will not be in better health than the sickest of its members, just as a chain is only as strong as its weakest link. Let us not wait for our fellow-Christians, or the church, to show love in its various forms towards us. Let us love our brothers with the love of Christ, let us love the church as Christ has loved it; then the peace of Christ will reign in our hearts and consequently in the whole body.

But here Paul may well realize how hard it is for the Christian to fulfil his calling and to put such absolute love into practice. So he quickly adds this extra thought: '**Be thankful.**' If it seems impossible for us to give, to give ourselves, to sacrifice ourselves for others, to show towards everyone, at all times, that compassion, kindness, humility, gentleness and patience — in short that love which is tolerant and forgiving, let us begin by 'being thankful'. If we find it hard to give, let us at least be grateful for what we have received. That is the first step in learning to love; it means to let go of one's independence and self-importance; it means to declare one's solidarity with others, to establish relationships; it means to weave the fabric of perfect unity. Being able to give thanks *from the heart* does much for unity and peace in the church.

17.
Christian worship

Please read Colossians 3:16–17

The Christian's new life is hidden in God, but it comes to light in a continual shedding of his evil nature and a simultaneous putting-on of the virtues inspired by God's love in his heart.

This process happens within the framework of the local church. For God in his wisdom has decided that our sanctification should come about with the help of our fellow-Christians. He could have chosen another way and sometimes we are sorry he did not. We should prefer God's gifts to come to us direct from him, not through other people (who are often so tactless!) — then we should not be in their debt! We should prefer to be indebted only to God! But that is not the way things are. By God's deliberate choice, sanctification is a collective process taking place in a community and, apart from special circumstances, the Christian's way to sanctification is in company with other Christians and with their help.

May God help us to understand his plan and be obedient to it with the humility which will become the hard but inevitable rule.

Collective worship

In collective worship there should be a place for three activities: preaching, sharing and singing. **'Let the word of Christ dwell in you richly as you teach and admonish one another with all wisdom, and as you sing psalms,**

**hymns and spiritual songs with gratitude [A.V. 'grace']
in your hearts to God.**'

These three forms of worship should not necessarily all
take place in the Sunday service — anyway, this would not
always be possible — but they should appear somewhere in
the church's life. The activities organized during the week
should allow time for these different aspects of worship, and
to them must be added prayer.

The Word of Christ is given first place: 'Let the *word of Christ*
dwell in you richly.' Reading it, proclaiming it, explaining it,
considering its implications, all this should form the basis of
worship. This proclamation of the Word of God was restored
by the Reformation to its proper place at the centre of
worship.

In some evangelical circles more emphasis is placed on
adoration than on preaching, which tends to be neglected.
But there cannot be true worship acceptable to God without
knowledge of his will; there can be no real spiritual life without divine revelation, the Word of Christ.

Paul has shown us that the Christian life is 'Christ in us'.
However, as he has already pointed out (1:24–28), Christ's
presence in us does not come about through a mystical *experience* but through biblical *teaching*. The Word of Christ, faithfully preached, must, by the action of the Spirit who inspired
it, gradually form in the Christian the likeness and character
of Jesus Christ: 'My dear children, for whom I am again in
the pains of childbirth until Christ is formed in you...!'
(Gal. 4:19). 'Christ in us': this is the Word of Christ *in* and
among us, unfolding all its riches, inspiring true worship and
developing genuine Christian lives.

Worship cannot be meaningful, intelligent or spiritual
(that is, in accordance with the Spirit) if this Word does not
occupy the central place when we gather together. What God
wishes to say to man is always more important than what
man can bring to him.

Preaching is much criticized today and the sermon is out

of favour — sometimes with good reason because of its lack of substance — but it can by no means be replaced by discussion or sharing in fellowship, however popular these may be. They have an important place, it is true, but must not exclude the solemn proclamation of the Word of God.

'*Teach and admonish one another* with all wisdom...' This instruction of Paul's suggests *free and spontaneous relationships*: Bible studies, mutual encouragement and correction, the sharing of experiences.

Here the Word of Christ has individual and practical repercussions. The preaching of the Word should not be vague and theoretical but should have practical relevance for life: the life of the church and the life of the Christian. The Word of Christ is the light which is to shine on life: to teach and put right, to instruct in the faith and to correct so as to lead to repentance.

We should notice that teaching and correction are not the monopoly of pastors; they are the duty of all church members. We are all personally responsible for our brothers, for showing each other where we are going wrong and building each other up. If we reject the notion of a separate 'clergy', it implies that we all accept responsibility for our brothers, taking upon ourselves the task of discipline which is the inevitable duty of the church. One frequently comes across those who staunchly support democracy when its privileges are to be enjoyed, such as taking part in decision-making. But this enthusiasm evaporates when they are faced with the attendant responsibilities, and many evade them by shifting them on to others when difficulties arise and order has to be reestablished. (What is true in the political sphere is also true in the church!) 'Teach and admonish one another.' This is true democracy! Let us play our part sincerely, faithfully, with the wisdom which God grants generously to those who claim it for this ministry.

Then there is a third element in worship: *singing*. Paul uses three words to stress his point: '*psalms, hymns and spiritual songs'*. The church's worship should be the outpouring of man's spontaneous response to God. This is why the Word of Christ, which encourages and rebukes, also makes the heart break forth into song, which embraces a whole range of feelings — praise and thanksgiving, humility and repentance, faith and hope.

Christ's presence in the hearts of Christians shows itself in hymns, the special language of worship. The Word of God, when faithfully preached, must touch not only the mind and conscience but also the heart. It cannot leave people unmoved and cold. If what is preached is really the Word of Christ it will lead quite naturally to song.

The Psalms of the Bible were composed in order to be sung, and they are still often the best expression of our feelings of wonder, praise and adoration of God. To express the same feelings we also have hymns, the songs of praise to God that Christians in every age have spontaneously composed or sung.

The last phrase, 'spiritual songs', probably sums up the two others, the adjective 'spiritual' distinguishing ordinary songs from hymns, which are addressed to God and inspired by the Spirit. This is what Paul stresses when he adds, 'singing *with grace in your hearts* to the Lord' (AV). The song on our lips should correspond to the song in our hearts — hearts which have known and experienced the grace of God and are full of its wonder. Hymns should be the response inspired by the Spirit himself to the grace of God revealed in the Word of Christ. So, preaching the Word and sharing in fellowship overflow naturally into adoration, and when these three elements are present the church is worshipping in spirit and in truth.

Everyday worship

But this collective worship is only a moment in the continuous worship which the Christian offers to God. For Paul broadens our vision: **'And whatever you do, whether in word or deed, do it all in the name of the Lord Jesus, giving thanks to God the Father through him.**' Here is true worship summed up in a sentence. No pious phrases! No sentimental or mystical outpourings! No lengthy instructions, no devotional handbook! Instead, a short, all-inclusive command without anything extraordinary or sensational about it, but which revolutionizes the whole of life, giving it purpose, meaning, dignity, greatness and holiness.

True worship is not intellectualism or sentimentality, nor is it an abstract theory, or a catalogue of petty pharisaical rules, but the reorientation of all the actions, words and thoughts which make up our ordinary everyday life. The true spiritual worship of a Christian is expressed at every moment of his existence. It is not limited to a few special times in the week, or some particular place, or a few pious words or gestures. It is not expressed only in setting aside a seventh of his time or a tenth of his income, but in the dedication of all his efforts, thoughts and words, all his time and all his possessions. This worship involves the dedication of his work and sleep, his health and food, his youth and old age, his natural abilities and his struggles, his joys and his sorrows. God has come into his life, into all of it, into its very centre; he has become its source and goal. He is everywhere and in everything.

When the Christian is working for his employer, he offers his work to God; when giving orders to those under him, he does it as serving God. When he talks to his neighbours, he does so knowing that God is present; when he sleeps or rests, he renews his strength to put it at God's disposal. When he helps the weak or the poor, it is God he is serving; when he studies, he does it to be more useful in God's service.

Everyone has a passion, a dominant interest in life: wealth, fame, politics, sport, music etc. For the Christian it is God whom he sees and serves everywhere. God fills his whole life, transforms his disappointments and failures, his grumbling and rebellion, his humiliations, his weariness, sleeplessness or poverty into songs of thankfulness: 'Whatever you do, whether in word or deed, do it all in the name of the Lord Jesus, giving thanks to God the Father through him.'

Yes, both collective and everyday worship should be a thankful, joyful, resounding, overflowing response to God's grace, to the riches and abundance which the Christian has found in Christ. Can we say that our worship in church, and also at work, at school, in the shop, in the kitchen or in our armchair, is really an expression of such thankfulness?

18.
The gospel and the family

Please read Colossians 3:18–21

Paul continues to follow up the implications of the new principle of life which he set out at the beginning of the practical part of his letter (3:1–4), and he now leads us into some thorny problems. They are as difficult today as they must have been then. The relationships between men and women, husbands and wives, parents and children, have always been live issues. We may think women's liberation and the greater freedom of young people are phenomena of our own times and, some will add, of the 'last days', the end of the world. This is not so[1].

From time to time, in one place or another, the unrest rises to fever pitch, but the underlying evil of which it is a symptom is as old as the world itself. In our present-day society we may well be going through one of those crises which will eventually succumb to the accumulated pressures of habits and attitudes of mind. But this unrest is an alarm signal

[1] For example, this is what was happening in the second century B.C.: 'now that the terror was over, there was less thought for the gods and much for finery. So when there was talk of repealing the Oppian Law (named after Oppius, the Roman Tribune who, after the disastrous defeat at Cannae in 216, had placed restrictions on the Roman women's use of jewellery, fine clothes and other luxuries), the noble ladies of Rome gathered in a large crowd. They filled the Via Sacra, the streets and the squares; they swarmed into the Forum, requesting politely or demanding imperiously the right to wear finery. They attacked the Oppian Law with the same spirit as that of their brothers or husbands when scaling the fortresses of Macedonia. Two tribunes who were trying to veto the repeal of the law, did not dare to brave the storm; they took refuge in their houses, where the ladies held them captive' (Aderer, *Revue des cours littéraires*, quoted by P. Guiraud, *Lectures historiques* p. 77).

which must be taken seriously. It would be just as dangerous to close our eyes to the reality of the underlying evil, as all down the ages some conservative thinkers have done, as it would be to join the revolutionaries (who have also been present in every period of history) in rushing into violent solutions. What should the Christian attitude be?

A new mentality

It is not always easy to discern God's voice amid the tumult of the world. Does the way we see things come from God, or from our own temperament, education, environment, race or sex? This is a question we have to face constantly. The answer is never easy, never obvious, never final.

Is our interpretation of the Bible that of the Spirit who inspired it? Do we not all too often understand God's words through minds as yet unrenewed? We must remember that sin has distorted, and still distorts, both the way we understand the Scriptures and the way we see the world. That is why 'the renewing of [our] mind' (Rom. 12:2) is a continuous work of God's Spirit to which we must constantly submit, so that we may be able to distinguish God's will from our own human feelings.

This is particularly necessary because the problem before us arouses strong feelings and because the Christian answer *seems* obvious. The Christian attitude must be neither conservative by force of habit nor revolutionary by reaction, but biblical and spiritual. What this attitude is we are aiming to discover in studying Paul's very brief words of advice to the Colossians. We shall try to keep to these, for to do full justice to such a question would necessitate a study of far wider scope and would involve consideration of all the biblical data, which is not our purpose here.

The husband–wife relationship

'**Wives, submit to your husbands, as is fitting in the Lord. Husbands, love your wives and do not be harsh with them**.' Note that Paul is not dealing in this passage with the general question of woman in society but with that of the wife within the family. The wife's attitude towards her husband will clearly have an influence on the social or cultural life of them both, but Paul has already spoken of that to the Corinthians (1 Cor. 7; 11; 14).

Paul may appear to be giving men the advantage and keeping the women in their traditional place as inferiors. But we must not be too influenced by first impressions. This is where we need to discard an outlook coloured by the world and to get close to the mind of the Spirit which emerges from the Scriptures as a whole. First of all, we must put these words back into their time and appreciate the explosive power of the gospel in the oppressive society of the first century, in particular for women and slaves. The proclamation of the equality of Jew and Greek, freeman and slave, man and woman (Gal. 3:28) set off a revolutionary ferment capable of provoking terrible counter-reactions. Paul's appeals for moderation, self-control, patience, love, are therefore very understandable. People's mentalities, even those of Christians, cannot be changed overnight.

At a time of social crisis and emancipation in which the woman suddenly regains a place of honour and equality at her husband's side[2], she may be tempted to insist arrogantly on her newly gained rights in relation to her husband and to dispute his authority. For his part, the husband is likely to get exasperated when his wife thus asserts her personality and freedom. Hence the twofold exhortation: 'Wives, submit to your husbands, as is fitting in the Lord. Husbands, love your wives and do not be harsh to them.'

[2] Peter goes so far as to tell husbands to 'grant honour' to their wives (NASB), just as he urged the Christians to 'honour the king'.

Indeed, the great principle of the gospel that all people — men and women — have full equality before God, runs the risk of stirring up the kind of disorder which the apostle rightly feared at the outset of Christianity (2:5; 1 Cor. 14:33, 40; 2 Thess. 3:11, AV), unless it is accompanied by personal discipline. The honour and credibility of the gospel and the harmony of the home are at stake.

The freedom of the Spirit which is the sign of spiritual maturity is one of self-discipline and love. Such freedom leaves no room for the flesh. It is when the wife is in full possession of her freedom[3] and can affirm her complete equality with her husband, that she joyfully submits to him. If this equality and freedom are absent, such submission has no more meaning or moral value. Submission without freedom and love would be a denial of the gospel and the Christian ideal of marriage. To give up one's rights is the privilege of freedom and an expression of love (1 Cor. 8); it is the condition of true possession: whoever loses his life will find it (Matt. 10:39).

But the man should not be too pleased with himself, or take advantage of the situation. His partner's willingness to obey — in what is good, right and wise, of course — gives him no authority to dominate her, still less to make her 'pay' for the restoration of her rights by his bad temper. Far from it! When she freely offers her love in renunciation, he should respond with a love which gives and is ready to make sacrifices, without bitterness or reluctance. Realizing the equal dignity of his companion and knowing that her freedom has been restored in Christ, he should not experience any feeling of frustration or any longing for lost superiority.

Besides, as in the previous case, is it not the glory of love to be humble? Did not Jesus show that humility, with which all of us, men and women, should clothe ourselves, consists in regarding others as better than ourselves? Did he not

[3] Writing on a parallel theme, Peter says that man's submission to authority takes place in complete and true freedom (1 Peter 2:13–17).

prove that love leads us to give up our legitimate rights and privileges, freely to empty ourselves, to humble ourselves so as to serve others? (Phil. 2:2–8.) Did he not turn upside down all generally accepted ideas (unfortunately they are still part of our Christian mentality) about the role of a leader or the concept of power? 'You know that the rulers of the Gentiles lord it over them, and their high officials exercise authority over them. Not so with you. Instead, whoever wants to become great among you must be your servant, and whoever wants to be first must be your slave' (Matt. 20:25–27). That is true greatness. That is the expression of real love which, both in the home and in the church, is mutual submission (Eph. 5:2). From now on it is in this perspective that the traditional ideas of the wife's submission and the husband's authority must be understood within the Christian home.

To sum up, submission is not without love, nor is love without submission. Love is just as fitting for the woman as submission is for the man. So Paul's two instructions to the Colossians are in agreement, though each probably stresses the weak point, the particular temptation, of wife or husband[4]. Their purpose is to establish or build up the harmony of the home, not to set up a hierarchy within it. By acknowledging the realities of human life (the confused state of society) and by correcting the reactions of the flesh (the woman's desire for independence, the man's retaliation), they aim to lead the couple towards the original ideal of 'one flesh' (Matt. 19:4–6), which will bring joy into the marriage and show the world the finest fruit of reconciliation produced by the gospel.

---

[4] These two words of advice do not sum up the whole ethic of marriage, any more than the whole ethic of bringing up children is represented by the one instruction: 'Fathers, do not embitter your children.' Perhaps they were more necessary in Paul's time; perhaps too they are the most necessary at all times.

The parent-child relationship

This harmony of the married couple will determine the harmony of the family; it is the relationship between husband and wife which conditions the relationship between parents and children. This co-operation, based on unity, not on status, is reflected in the upbringing of the children. **'Children, obey your parents in everything, for this pleases the Lord. Fathers, do not embitter [NASB, 'exasperate']your children, or they will become discouraged.'**

Though it is the fathers who have to be careful not to exasperate their children, the children owe obedience to the 'parents', not just the father. This detail needs to be pointed out, because it must have been quite remarkable in Paul's time, although it may not surprise us today. It reminds us also, if we need reminding, that the patriarchal system, which is sometimes held up as an example, is by no means a Christian idea.

Let us note, too, that the wife's relationship to her husband is not the same as that of the children to their parents. While the wife is called to a free act in love — 'Submit' — the children are given a command — 'Obey'. The slaves are similarly told to obey their masters. In the last two cases there is a suggestion of a difference of status which is absent in the first[5].

Children owe obedience to their parents. Paul has in mind no exception to the rule: 'in *everything*'. The child must learn to obey from the very early stages of his life. It is not when he is five, ten or fifteen years old that his parents should begin to worry about it — by then it will be too late! This discipline, which a child needs as much as his food and education, will, if absorbed steadily in an atmosphere of love and joy, stand him in good stead when he comes under all kinds

[5] Hugedé also points out that 'submit' is in the middle voice in the Greek, whilst 'obey' is in the active. The first command is felt not to represent a master's point of view, but that of someone freely consenting to it because, under the combined influence of love and the Spirit, he or she wishes to do so.

of restrictions at school and later on at work (Prov. 22:6). If his character has not been toughened in this way he will not be equipped to meet life's hardships and to submit to authorities, employers — and indeed to the Lord himself; he may well find things difficult or become rebellious as he grows up into society or the church. Everything in life is bound up together; life cannot be divided into compartments.

It is interesting that Paul asks for the child's obedience not by referring to the law — which he has in mind, however (Eph. 6:1–3) — but by showing that 'this pleases the Lord'. We can certainly appeal to this motive early in a child's life. In this way he will learn how he should behave at the same time as beginning to see the fatherly character of God. Furthermore, when one day he thinks for himself and discovers his parents' weaknesses, perhaps even their unworthiness, he will be able to go on respecting and obeying them not because they deserve it, but because this pleases God. If, however, his obedience has been linked to their authority rather than God's approval, it might have given way to contempt and rebellion.

Finally, a word to the fathers: 'Fathers, *do not exasperate your children*, that they may not lose heart' (NASB). Surely Paul cannot be singling out the father as having sole authority in the children's upbringing: as we have seen, they should obey both parents. Is he not rather picking on a failing common to fathers in every age? Few adults understand young people's attitudes today. (Whether these are good or bad is not for us to discuss here.) The mother, following her nature, tries to temporize and smooth things over. But the father, who may not always be as sensitive or as close to his child because of his work, is likely to intervene more sharply and cut short those endless and sometimes incoherent discussions which are nevertheless an important part of growing up[6].

---

[6] Let us not forget the law of growth so well illustrated by Jesus' parable (Mark 4:28).

Relationships between the generations, which have always been difficult, are made worse today by the pervasive and seductive propaganda constantly bombarding young people. They cannot ignore it, and their attitude at home is sure to annoy their parents and to provoke them at times to react in a scornful or violent way — especially the father, who wishes to assert his authority and impose his point of view. In so doing, the parents may discourage some high-minded feeling which has been clumsily expressed, or break the bond which would have given stability to the developing personality of the young adult. We who are parents need now more than ever to heed what God is saying in this letter which he inspired. We need much self-control, firmness, love and wisdom to make a good job of bringing up our children.

This advice of Paul's, so brief and simple, will always be the key to harmony between husband and wife; this in turn is the secret of harmony in the family, and consequently in society and in the church. If all of us — wives, husbands, children — are faithful in the little things of family life, God will entrust us with greater things. Meanwhile, the inexpressible joys that God will give us each day as we carry out our tasks will be our greatest reward.

19.
The gospel and relationships at work

Please read Colossians 3:22–4:1

A few thoughts on relationships at work from a Christian viewpoint ('in Christ') end Paul's survey of the transformations that the gospel brings about in people's hearts and lives. Here again, as in the previous chapter, we must take into account the social set-up in which he was expressing his thoughts and advice. Conditions in the family and at work were not what they are now — at any rate in Western Europe! So, as we try to understand what the Bible says, we must allow for certain discrepancies.

As Christian employees today, we are anxious to know how to act towards our employers, and as Christian employers we want to know how we should act towards our employees. The biblical answer is not all that simple.

The gospel yesterday

We must first remember that here we are not talking about twentieth-century employees, workers or civil servants, but slaves. At that time a slave[1] belonged entirely to his master.

[1] 'The slave was his maters's property: in himself he was nothing and had nothing. That was the principle; and every possible implication of it went to make up the conditions of life common to all slaves in most countries. At all periods of history and in all situations in life they were subject to this absolute authority which decreed their fate with both harshness and indifference. When they were strong in body and mind they were condemned at the whim of authority either to hard work or to vice. Work was for the rougher; vice was for the more delicate, who were well looked after for the master's pleasure and, when he was tired of them, put to prostitution for his profit. When too young or too old to work, they were left to themselves in weakness or sickness: the children grew up completely uncared for; the old often died in extreme poverty and were sometimes abandoned by the roadside' (Wallon, *Histoire de l'esclavage*, quoted by Lightfoot, *op. cit.*, p. 321).

He could not offer his labour for a wage, nor change his employer as we are free to do nowadays; he could not demand
higher wages, better hours, better conditions of work, or
longer and more frequent holidays; and he had no civic
rights at all. He often had no alternative but to obey. It was
the best way to avoid an even harsher situation.

'Slaves, obey your earthly masters in everything.' Is
Paul suggesting they should simply resign themselves, like
the Stoic philosophers who submitted to everything that
happened and refused to desire or seek anything better?
Strangely enough, around that time there was born in
Hierapolis, which Paul mentions later (4:13) — thus not far
from Colosse and Laodicea — a slave who was to become a
famous philosopher: Epictetus. The story goes that one day
he said to his master who was torturing him, 'You are going
to break my leg.' When this happened, the slave merely said,
'I told you so!'[2]

Is Paul preaching this kind of resignation to the Christian
slaves? That is how he is sometimes interpreted and Christianity is accused in particular of having hindered progress
and kept the masses in slavery. We are familiar with the
maxim: 'Religion is the opium of the people' — in other
words, by holding out the hope of heaven, the gospel gets
unhappy men to accept anything here on earth.

Actually, Paul rather lays himself open to this criticism
when he promises, **'You know that you will receive an
inheritance from the Lord as a reward**.' This is true!
Indeed, he even goes much further than the Stoic's simple
resignation when he writes, **'Obey your earthly masters in
everything: and do it not only when their eye is on you
and to win their favour, but with sincerity of heart and
reverence for the Lord. Whatever you do, work at it
with all your heart, as working for the Lord, not for
men**.'

---

[2] This may only be a legend, but it expresses well the attitude of the future
philosopher.

But let us examine more closely the effects of the gospel in the master–slave relationship of yesterday and the employer–employee relationship of today. The sorry life of the Christian slave is unexpectedly filled with light, for the gospel has given it meaning. Christ has entered a wretched man's life and he is now united with Christ. He is 'one with him'. He becomes rich with Christ's riches, free with his freedom. His heart fills with hope and he knows, in Paul's words, that 'when Christ, who is [his] life, appears, then [he] also will appear with him in glory' (3:4). As he discovers new meaning for his miserable existence, and the hope which this meaning brings, his slavery is transformed. His attitude is nothing like the austere resignation of the Stoic. Paul's words to him are no sick humour, no cruel cynicism, they are becoming real in his life! Behind his dreaded master he discovers Christ. In serving him he serves Christ, his true Lord, his only Lord (1 Cor. 8:5, 6).

No, it is not resignation, but victory despite fetters, light amid endless night, joy in privation. Revolt gives way to devotion, hatred to respect, curses are answered with blessings. Bitter slavery is *transfigured* until the time comes for it to be conquered — not by violence but by love, not by the overthrow of the appalling established order but by the transformation of men's hearts.

Our present world, so accustomed to violence, accuses Paul of helping to perpetuate an intolerable situation, of collaborating with the establishment, the iniquitous system which had a vested interest in keeping slavery going. Today's protests certainly appear to have some justification. Not only did Paul apparently not raise his voice against this evil, but he wrote his letter to a church where various members were slave-owners without a word of reproach to them. We know the name of one of them: Philemon. What is more, Paul sends the letter by a slave, Onesimus (4:7–9), who had run away from his master and been converted in prison through Paul. Instead of helping Onesimus to complete his escape and gain his emancipation, the apostle sends him back to slavery under his old master in Colosse; he puts him back in bonds˙ without even condemning this cruel practice. These are the facts which revolt us in the twentieth century.

And yet, it was that very gospel which was to shake the society of the time and slowly but surely erode slavery. This gospel of peace, with its call to submission, obedience and love, its call to render good for evil, is a revolutionary power greater than all the violence of men. In our time Martin Luther King has proved the effectiveness of non-violent protest.

In a few well-chosen words, Paul turns to the masters. He does not explicitly denounce the current practice of slavery, but he undermines its foundations. It is noteworthy that he does not require pity or sympathy. He demands much more. He goes to the heart of the matter, asking not for favours but justice and fairness: '**Masters, provide your slaves with what is right and fair**.'

He reminds the Christian masters, themselves prisoners of their times, that a slave is a man and not a thing, having not only duties but rights. He stresses this by adding, '**You know that you also have a Master in heaven**.' Thus he places the slave on the same human level as his master. While the slave has a master to whom he is answerable, the latter too has a master, God, to whom he is fully accountable. These few words, which seem quite normal to us today, were the tiny seed which was to grow and lead to the abolition of slavery[3].

The gospel today

While the situation that Paul was familiar with is still an

---

[3] To get a more complete idea of Paul's attitude to slavery, we should follow his argument in the letter to Philemon. We find in it no general demand for slaves' rights, nor a formal command to the master, but the irresistible pressure of love. Onesimus' emancipation was to be a spontaneous action coming from Philemon's heart.

unpleasant reality in many countries, relationships between employers and employees have greatly improved as far as we are concerned. What do Paul's instructions mean for our own society, in which the employer is no longer the brutal master, nor the employee the slave of former times? Should the worker put up with any conditions, any pay, any work which may be imposed on him? Should he 'obey in everything' the orders he gets from those in charge? Should the Christian, by servile obedience, support the interests of management against those of the work force? Has he not the right, if not the duty, to go to the help of the oppressed and needy, to fight the flagrant injustices of present-day society (as indeed of any society: Eccl. 3:16; 4:1; 5:8), such as the exploitation of man by man? Or should he remain passive, as this letter would seem to suggest?

It is not an easy question and Paul does not answer it exactly; as we have seen, he deals with a particular case — the relationship between master and slave. Today the employee is no longer his employer's slave, whatever may be said! He is not tied for life to the same employer; often he even has means of putting pressure on him. The state grants him rights. Should he use them? Can he take part in industrial action and withdraw his labour to obtain satisfaction? It does not seem that we can condemn such legally permitted action by quoting Paul's words: 'Slaves, obey your earthly masters in everything . . .' For Paul, who instructed that the authorities should be obeyed, also resisted them sometimes. The Christian is a responsible citizen who knows how to put his obedience to God before his obedience to men[4]. The fact that there are rights is a credit to our society; however, the Christian should use them according to the Lord's will. Following Jesus Christ's example, Paul and the other apostles resisted the authorities so as to obey God and not their own selfish interests. We must be careful not to confuse God's cause with our own ambitions, greed and jealousy!

[4] The instruction to obey the authorities is not unconditional, despite certain traditional interpretations of Romans 13:1–7.

The Christian can never remain unmoved by the injustices of this world. Sometimes his protest will involve him in a painful and costly struggle. He has no right to leave it to the world alone to fight for justice. The hope of a heavenly kingdom of justice and peace must not excuse him from fighting for just causes on earth. The *eternal* kingdom to which he belongs embraces earth as well as heaven, both the present order of things and that which is to come.

But the weapons for this conflict cannot always be the weapons of the world. The Christian cannot identify with violence. Any just cause he defends will be better served if he does his work today in the spirit that Paul urged upon the slaves of the first century. Honesty, loyalty and conscientiousness will add weight to any just protest. Even an employer's unfairness cannot make it right for a Christian employee to be dishonest or careless: '**Anyone who does wrong will be repaid for his wrong, and there is no favouritism**.'

If the apostle demanded such behaviour from a slave towards a brutal master, how much more does the gospel require it of the employee of today! Nothing can ever justify evil — not even evil itself. Our honour as Christians — and what is more, God's honour — is at stake. At work it should be obvious that we are Christians, not only by our words but also by a life beyond reproach: 'Obey your earthly masters in everything, not only when their eye is on you and to win their favour, but with sincerity of heart and reverence for the Lord.'

Only by discovering and serving God in our work shall we be able to act with such joy and serenity. Work is divinely ordained, even if working conditions are often far from perfect. As we work, let us realize that we are fulfilling our spiritual calling, and let us serve Christ: 'Whatever you do, work at it with all your heart, as working for the Lord, not for men.'

The attitude of Christian employers remains to be

examined. Their duty seems more clear-cut but may not be
so easy in practice, as they are not always free agents; they,
too, must often comply with requirements over which they
have no control. '**Masters, provide your servants with
what is right and fair, because you know that you also
have a Master in heaven**.' They should be aiming, not at
unfair egalitarianism or idealistic charity, but at justice and
fairness. What a fine ideal for a Christian employer! It is,
however, an uphill struggle with many disappointments, and
more chances of being misunderstood and despised than of
being praised and respected! Nevertheless this is the hard yet
worthwhile task to which an employer is called, under the
eye of his sovereign Master, who will understand and reward
him.

Justice is at the heart of everything divine, of all that is
Christian, yet Protestant Christianity has often emphasized
order at the expense of justice, heaven at the expense of the
world, the soul at the expense of the body. Today we are
witnessing the inevitable reaction: a Christianity that is
purely social, even political and revolutionary.

There is something revolutionary about the gospel, it is
true. This does not mean, however, that it incites to violence,
but that by changing the individual's heart it transforms his
outlook on everything, including his idea of relationships at
work. Slavery was not abolished by Paul, nor by the protests
or revolts of the victims of this social scourge. But the gospel
transformed both the slave and the slave-owner into servants
or slaves of God. It is not class conflict, but the reconciliation
of social classes in submission to the one and only Master in
brotherly love, which can really abolish this most revolting
evil of all time.

Let us 'seek first [God's] kingdom and his righteousness'
here and now, in a society which rejects its standards and
despises its ways. Let us put its spirit into practice despite
the derision which the apparent inadequacy of its resources
will surely arouse. As employers and workers, let us freely

and joyfully live out God's requirements in our relationships with each other: justice, truth, honesty, loyalty, willingness. Like this we shall live the kingdom of God on earth here and now, while preparing ourselves for the kingdom to come. 'Blessed are those who hunger and thirst for righteousness, for they will be filled.'

20.
Prayer and witness

Please read Colossians 4:2–6

The fact that we spend the larger part of our life in the family circle or at work makes these two spheres our first mission-field. Both areas are very difficult to witness in; they are particularly resistant to the spirit of the gospel, because in them the old nature and the influences of the world around tend to make their presence felt openly and without inhibition. So, although Paul's exhortation to prayer and witness no doubt goes beyond relationships in the family and at work, we should not too hastily assume that it has no connection with the instructions in the preceding verses.

Prayer to God and witness to men are not optional extras or luxuries in the Christian life. We cannot approach this twofold calling as amateurs or dilettanti: it must fill our life, it is our life. For we are saved to serve, to devote to God, either directly or in serving our neighbour, all our strength and all our time, whatever may be our circumstances, work, talents or handicaps.

Prayer

Paul begins with general advice about prayer, and then gives his brothers in Colosse a specific matter for intercession. **'Devote yourselves to prayer, keeping alert in it with an attitude of thanksgiving'** (NASB). Here we see three characteristics of prayer: it must be persistent, alert and thankful.

The persistence spoken of here does not mean repeatedly

asking for the same thing until God answers our prayer, even though that advice is sometimes given (Luke 18:1–8). It means rather to 'cling' to prayer, to pray continually and constantly, as Paul reminds us elsewhere: 'Pray continually' (1 Thess. 5:17). We should not think of prayer as an occasional thought, or as a last resort in an emergency, when all human help has failed, but as a natural reflex, a kind of automatic reaction (such as breathing), a permanent attitude, a habit of daily life. Prayer is no other than the expression of the Christian's fellowship with his God; the more real and conscious this fellowship is, the more frequent and persistent prayer will be.

But prayer is also the channel bringing God's life into our lives, nourishing and deepening our communion with him. Just as breathing is sustained by life and life is renewed by breathing, so prayer depends on our communion with God, and this communion depends in turn on prayer. Prayer and life, prayer and communion, all are inseparable. This is why Paul reminds us: *'Devote yourselves to prayer.'*

Unfortunately a danger is latent in every habit, even the best, and this is evident in the case of prayer: prayer may become mechanical, lifeless and cold. This is why the apostle adds a phrase that is rich in meaning: *'Keeping alert in it'* (NASB). This can be understood either as a call to 'stay awake, be vigilant while praying', or as meaning that prayer will help us to keep alert: 'It is through prayer that you will remain vigilant.'

How sad it is to think that prayer, which is a wonderful reality, can be just a string of words, a series of empty, lifeless phrases, a well-adjusted mechanism which does not drive anything! We may smile at Eastern prayer-wheels or the litanies of some religions, but have we never addressed to God 'meaningless repetition', prayers that were lifeless because our heart was not in them, because they no longer expressed communion but the absence of it? Let us pray with persistence, but also watchfully; let us not become lethargic when we pray, but let us keep awake with the help of prayer.

Lastly, prayer should be *thankful*. Thankfulness, which is mentioned so often in this letter (1:12; 2:7; 3:15, 17), is what prayer, as Paul understands it, should lead to. Thankfulness flows naturally, spontaneously, from a life of prayer. Prayer is our means of talking to God, but it is also God's means of speaking to us: lighting our way, leading us, consoling us. Prayer is not a one-way street, as is so often thought. God has many more things to tell us through prayer than we have to say to him.

And so, through this communion, step by step, we discover God's plan for us, we enter into it, and then we see the real meaning of our lives. All the events in our life, whether happy or unhappy, small or great, take on meaning and become an element in our happiness. Thus a prayerful life becomes a thankful life, in which each little circumstance is transformed into a reason for praise. The habit of prayer becomes the habit of thanksgiving. This is what transforms life and makes the face light up. This is the Christian life!

Among the many subjects for continual prayer, Paul mentions one in particular: '**Pray for us, too, that God may open a door for our message, so that we may proclaim the mystery of Christ, for which I am in chains**.' He urges the Colossians to pray for him and his fellow-workers, probably Timothy and Epaphras.

A pastor is the last person we expect to need support in prayer. He is always giving, he is full of spiritual strength! (This is a very widely held idea — outside ministerial circles!) Yet Jesus himself needed the prayers of his friends (Matt. 26:38). How much more do we, his weak disciples!

Very often it is the pastor, more than other people, who feels the need to be renewed by God, because he is exposed more than others to the routine of duties, to weariness, lethargy, discouragement, wandering thoughts and all kinds of temptations. 'Pray for us, too!' was Paul's earnest request; and for two things in particular: that God would provide opportunities to proclaim the mystery of Christ, the gospel, and help him to make the most of these opportunities.

Paul was in prison. He wanted to use this situation to preach the gospel where otherwise it would have no chance of being proclaimed. He was probably not asking for God to open the prison door: that was not the most important thing, although some may think so. He was asking that God would open the doors of circumstances, the doors of hearts, so that he would be able to take full advantage of his captivity. So we see that prayer leads quite naturally to witness, to which Paul turns next.

Witness

Fellowship with God inevitably implies fellowship with men. It is important to note that prayer does not shut the Christian away in a selfish private dialogue with God, it is always sending him out into the world. Prayer becomes witness and witness turns into prayer. They are two aspects of the Christian's fellowship with God, of the same balanced spiritual life. **'Be wise in the way you act towards outsiders; make the most of every opportunity. Let your conversation be always full of grace, seasoned with salt, so that you may know how to answer everyone.'**

Witness, we notice, is presented as *answering*. This is certainly very significant and ought to guide us in our approach to those who do not yet belong to the church (*'outsiders'*) and, more generally, in our thinking about evangelism.

The reply must be personalized: 'to answer everyone'. This is certainly an important feature of the gospel: it has to be lived according to the uniqueness of personality of each Christian. The life of the Spirit is not stereotyped. The same Spirit finds expression in countless different ways (1 Cor. 12:4 –13). The gospel is not only the answer to the needs of the world, but also to the particular needs of each individual.

But an answer presupposes a question. Now, what is more likely to make 'outsiders' want to ask questions than a 'different' life, a way of living that cannot be explained by the usual worldly motives, aims and standards? A genuine, radiant Christian life is sure to make the many people who find no satisfaction in their own lives think and perhaps ask questions.

We can therefore understand why Paul stresses the Christian's conduct: *'Be wise in the way you act towards outsiders.'* The way we act towards others will either provide a natural opening for witness or else it will shut the door. A holy life is certainly the best sermon, but how right Paul is to emphasize *wisdom*! How many 'holy' lives have left those who were really searching standing 'outside'! How many 'blameless' Christians have lived out only God's *'righteousness'*, without the wisdom of love! The holiness which does in fact *separate* the Christian from the world could *isolate* him, cut him off completely from all contact with it, so making any witness impossible.

Wisdom is a quality of life which should permeate our relationships with others, for it is 'first of all pure; then peace-loving, considerate, submissive, full of mercy and good fruit, impartial and sincere' (James 3:17). Peter confirms this by linking gentleness and respect with holiness and a clear conscience when witnessing to those who disparage Christian conduct (1 Peter 3:17–18). Wisdom must show through in our lives as well as in our words.

But we should not let our witness be paralysed by the thought of all these demands. So Paul adds straight away, *'Make the most of every opportunity.'* Wisdom is not the enemy of *action*, but prompts us to take advantage of every moment God gives us, to seek every opportunity to present the gospel to those still 'outside', who do not yet know the light and warmth of the hope it offers. No one is stopping us from dreaming of more favourable conditions and trying to create them, but meanwhile let us make the most of any small openings there may be now (Eccl. 11:4 – 6; cf 3:1–8).

Wisdom does not mean the Christian should do nothing because he feels inadequate, it gives him guidance in the delicate work of witnessing. Now, witness is inevitably coloured by the personality of whoever is trying to present the truth. Depending on who is speaking, either the stern or the joyful side of the gospel can show through. It is difficult not to give a false impression of it by unconsciously stressing either judgement or grace, which are really in perfect balance.

That is why Paul insists, *'Let your conversation be always full of grace and seasoned with salt.'* The gentleness of grace should not make salt lose its sharpness, nor should the sharpness of salt take away the gentleness of grace. Salt and grace should not neutralize but strengthen each other. From the bitterness of sin will spring the joy of forgiveness; the deeper the one, the fuller will be the other. The gospel condemns and heals, for it is judgement and grace. It pierces and consoles, for it is powerful and gentle. Let us then make every effort, even in spite of our temperament, to put across as faithfully as possible, through our attitude and words, a balanced gospel in all its power and beauty. Let our aim be to speak the truth in love (Eph. 4:15).

Do we need to point out that the grace which should be in our words is not mere pleasantness? What should come out in our witness is the grace of Christ himself. In the same way, the salt with which our words should be seasoned has nothing to do with the piquancy of conversation but the wholesomeness of truth.

Prayer and witness are two facets of the same life lived in the sight of God and men, two echoes of the same words spoken both to God and men. Prayer will lead us to witness, for to meet with God always brings us face to face with men. Witness will lead us back to prayer by making us conscious of the inadequacy of our words. Witness will give us reasons for being watchful in prayer, because by ourselves we shall feel too weak to carry the burdens of others. Prayer will give us wisdom in our witness because, confident that God is in full control, we shall not get over-anxious and will be freed from the very human temptation to be too insistent with other people.

21.
God and men

Please read Colossians 4:7–18

The only cure for errors in doctrine, or in the life of the
church or the Christian, is to preach Jesus Christ. Paul has
freely used this remedy throughout his letter: he has constantly given Jesus Christ the highest place and has held him
up as the only answer to all the problems facing the early
church.

He has shown us the person of Jesus: the perfect image of
God because he *is* God; the goal and Lord of the universe;
the Head of the church; the only mediator between God and
men; the source, inspiration and pattern of real Christian
life. 'You have been given fulness in Christ' for he is the
origin and substance of all things: this has been Paul's main
theme, the thread running through the whole letter.

But in the closing lines we are suddenly brought down
from these heights and find ourselves involved in personal
messages of little apparent interest. What is there for us in
these greetings and instructions addressed to friends of Paul
who are so distant from us, indeed quite unknown? Is this
how one of the books of God's Word should end? Why does
it not finish, like a good sermon, on a lofty note? Instead, it
brings us back to the down-to-earth realities which we know
so well and which sometimes seem unworthy of God. Are
these final words still part of the divine revelation? Most certainly! What is more, they have something to teach us about
it.

The Word of God and human history

In this case the Word of God takes the form of a letter — a

letter written by a man in special circumstances and ending, as might be expected, with a few personal messages, a letter like many others. God's Word does not always come as systematic teaching like the Mosaic law, the Sermon on the Mount or the great arguments of the Epistle to the Romans. It is usually bound up with the life of men, it comes to life in their life, it both shapes and uses their feelings. It is conveyed through human relationships and is expressed, as here, by simple greetings.

The last part of the epistle is not a postscript devoid of theological interest; it is just as much the Word of God as the great truths with their practical implications that have held our attention so far. In particular it reminds us that divine revelation does not belong to the realm of myth, that it is not a document fallen from heaven (like certain sacred writings of various man-made religions), but that it is set in a *geographical* context and woven into the *history* of the world — more precisely the history of individuals, some virtuous, others weak, some faithful, others cowardly.

We might be tempted to forget this when trying to understand and interpret God's message and apply it to our own time. Though its essence is eternal and universal, it finds concrete expression in time and place. This is certainly more noticeable in the epistles, especially their endings, than in the dogmatic writings; though even these are rarely uninfluenced by the social and religious context of the time[1]. Every part of the Bible was written to meet a precise situation in the world of that time before meeting the needs of men in every age.

And so, at the end of this Epistle to the Colossians, the Word of God comes in the form of simple greetings, signs of quite spontaneous relationships between man and man, between one church and another. It is present in the warm fel-

---

[1] Notably the Ten Commandments, which are indisputably universal in their content, but the precise form in which they are expressed reflects the points in time at which they were given (compare Exodus 20:1–17 with Deut. 5:6–21).

lowship between Paul, Epaphras, Mark, Aristarchus, Demas, Luke, Justus, Nympha, Archippus and others; between Ephesus, Rome, Colosse, Hierapolis and Laodicea. Here is no doctrinal intellectualism, but the growth of a network of friendships expressing God's love in human lives and proving that the gospel is real.

How amazing is the Word of God! How different from the theological and ethical treatises of men! It has actually taken on flesh and blood in men's destiny and in man's whole being: mind, heart, soul and body; in history's great moments and small insignificant events. For the gospel is a new life which permeates our whole existence and enables us to live in a quite ordinary yet quite different way. This is probably the reason why God preserved for us this letter, and especially these closing greetings, from among many other writings which he could have chosen.

The church of God — a gathering of men

In these lines we also have invaluable teaching about the church of God: we see it in its human reality, as it actually is.

The church is a gathering of people who would never have joined together or even met each other if God had not been at work, so unlike each other are they, so different in background, separated by language, race, social class and temperament. At that time there were Jews: Aristarchus, probably from Thessalonica, Mark the cousin of Barnabas, Jesus called Justus, of whom nothing is known. There were Greeks: Epaphras from Colosse, Luke the doctor (from Troas?) and Demas the Thessalonian. There were also educated men like Luke, freemen like Epaphras and slaves like Onesimus. All these men, of different nationalities, occupations and backgrounds, and with very different experiences of life, were united in one brotherhood and were forming a living bond of warm affection by their journeys, letters and prayers.

What joy to find among the names that of *Mark* who, through timidity or cowardice, had deserted Paul and Barnabas in Asia and had thus caused a disagreement between them! (Acts 15:37–39.) Mark, whom Paul had decided not to take with him again, was to stay faithfully, steadfastly at his side until the end. Paul speaks of him without bitterness here, for the past has been forgiven, and letters of recommendation restoring Mark's good name were even sent to the churches, asking them to receive him graciously. A weakness, a mistake, a failure are never irreparable: love always goes on hoping! So, in the church, we find former enemies reconciled and working together; love has done its work.

Demas on the other hand, who was to desert Paul soon after, was still with him, side by side with Mark who had let him down before (2 Tim. 4:10). Such is the church in its strength and weakness, its joys and sorrows, its encouragements and disappointments. The church of God is a gathering of very human people!

But we must not forget *Onesimus*, the runaway slave and thief, saved from his fate by God's grace, making amends by returning to his master (Philem. 10–18). The gospel has changed their old master-slave relationship and they are now two brothers about to meet in Colosse, when Onesimus gets back home with the precious letter addressed to Philemon.

Tax-collectors and Pharisees, masters and slaves, the educated and the ignorant, the cultured and the uncivilized — the church is not a closed group, an association like any other, it is neither middle class nor working class, nor aristocratic nor intellectual. The church of God is that living body, that rich and enriching variety of men and women of all backgrounds, redeemed and united to each other in Jesus Christ through God's grace.

Servants of God and servants of men

We must underline another fact which emerges from this

passage: these men in the service of God are at the same time whole-heartedly in the service of men.

There is *Tychicus*, '**a dear brother, a faithful minister and fellow-servant in the Lord**'. There is *Aristarchus* who devoted himself to looking after Paul during his captivity and who, together with Mark and Justus, '**worked for the kingdom of God**' and comforted the apostle in his time of testing. There is also *Epaphras*, '**a servant of Christ Jesus**', who, when far from his church, continued to wrestle in prayer for it and for its two sister churches in Hierapolis and Laodicea. Then there is *Luke*, caring for Paul's health, which was often under severe strain; he was also an evangelist and a trusted pastor. Several times he was given the responsibility of following up the apostle's work. Finally there is *Nympha*, in whose house the Laodicean church met.

It is clear from this long list that the apostle Paul's great work also become that of a whole team of capable men, united by the Spirit and dedicated to the kingdom of God. Paul did not suffer the isolation of some great men. He was helped, comforted and complemented by people of great worth. Far from creating a vacuum around him, his greatness acted like an irresistible magnet.

All these people were at the same time fully in the service of *God* and completely in the service of *men*. The knowledge that they were working for God in no way cut them off from men. To be close to God is also to be close to men. This sympathy is real and human: it is not only obedience to God, but the heart's response to the other person's need. It is not a 'good deed', but a selfless act springing irresistibly from a loving heart. Its 'horizontal' and 'vertical' dimensions merge into one.

This twofold call from God and men, and the total self-giving of God's servant in answer to this call, stand out very clearly in Paul's testimony: '**Epaphras, who is one of you, and a servant of Christ Jesus, sends greetings. He is always wrestling in prayer for you ... I vouch for him that he is working hard for you and for those at**

Laodicea and Hierapolis.' Epaphras kept in close touch with the problems of these churches and prayed for them in real suffering, the suffering that comes from love.

The evangelist, the pastor, the doctor — they are not content with bringing a message from God to a lost world; they join the battle, their hearts are full of compassion, and their whole being suffers for and with their fellow men.

God's revelation and man's solidarity

There is a final lesson to be learnt from the end of the Epistle to the Colossians. Though God can reveal himself to men directly, without any intermediary, he has often chosen to make himself known through Christian brothers: '**After this letter has been read to you, see that it is also read in the church of the Laodiceans and that you in turn read the letter from Laodicea**.' So Paul sent two letters, one to Colosse, the other to Laodicea. Each was intended to complement the other: the Colossians needed to know what God had to say to the Laodiceans, just as the Laodiceans needed to know what was God's message to the Colossians.

So knowledge of God is inseparable from human solidarity — the solidarity of churches and of Christians. In this divine principle we have protection against pride and also an obligation to work for unity; this applies equally to members of the same church and to the different churches.

Others need what God has taught us and we need what God has taught them. So we are all in the process of learning humility and love. 'What God has told me' must always be checked against what he has told someone else. Churches or Christians who depart from this principle of solidarity, refusing to hear what others have to say, are starting on the way to sectarianism and heresy. Let us accept to learn from one another, not so as to water down the teaching in God's Word, not to the extent of giving up all our principles, but to check if our faith is sound, to draw nearer to the truth while broadening our vision.

It is 'together with all the saints' (Eph. 3:18) that we can get to know God. This was the experience of Colosse and Laodicea. For we have reason to believe that the letter to the Ephesians was a circular letter and that one copy was addressed to Laodicea. So the letter to the Laodiceans which Paul mentions could be the same as that of which we can read another copy in the Epistle to the Ephesians, which the Holy Spirit has preserved for us among the books of the Bible[2]. The two letters, to the Ephesians and the Colossians, were thus intended to be complementary. And the teaching given to the Colossians about the person of Christ, for example, was to be complemented by that given to the Laodiceans about the church by our Epistle to the Ephesians.

The Colossians were entrusted with part of the truth, part of the divine revelation; the Laodiceans were given another. There is no doubt at all that today we have a far more complete knowledge of the things of God than these two churches, since we possess all the inspired writings of the Bible. But the principle remains: we still have much to learn from other people through whom God wishes to speak to us. We are not the sole, exclusive and definitive guardians of the truth. May our love for it move our hearts and minds to accept this principle of solidarity in humility and faithfulness, for the enrichment of ourselves and others.

The final word will be Paul's: **'Grace be with you.'** It repeats the same prayer, the same desire which opened the epistle: grace. Grace is the alpha and omega of God's work and revelation. May it also be the beginning and the end, the inspiration and the strength, of our whole lives. It is in Christ and through grace that we have 'been made complete'.

See Lightfoot, *op. cit.*, pp. 37, 242.

The hypothesis, let us note, is not that an Epistle to the Laodiceans should be substituted for the Epistle to the Ephesians, but that there was a circular letter, for which the Epistle to the Colossians may have been the occasion, taking up the same problem of the Christian attitude towards pagan mysticism but in more general terms.' N. Hugedé, *op. cit.*, p. 220.